Atlas of
WORLD WAR II

Atlas of
WORLD WAR II
Richard Natkiel

Text by Robin L Sommer
Introduction by S L Mayer

JG PRESS

Printed 2005 by
World Publications Group, Inc.
455 Somerset Avenuc
North Dighton, MA 07264
www.wrldpub.net

Printed in China by SNP Leefung Printers

*Page 1: Occupying German troops march
past the Arc de Triomphe, Paris, 1940.
Page 2-3: Italian troops on the Eastern
Front, 1942.
This page: US Marines at Iwo Jima plot
the position of a Japanese machine gun
post, February 1945.*

Contents

Introduction 6
Blitzkrieg 10
The War in Northern Waters 32
The Desert War and the Mediterranean 42
Soviet Ambitions Betrayed 64
The Course of Global Conflict: 1939-45 78
The Japanese Juggernaut 96
The Italian Campaign 108
Ebb Tide in the Pacific 120
Retaking Burma: The Forgotten War 138
Russia Finds Its Strength 148
Fortress Europe Overthrown 166
Index 190

Introduction

It has often been stated that World War II was part of a European Civil War that began in 1914 at the start of World War I. This is partly true. In Europe, at least, the two world wars were the two hideous halves of the Anglo-German controversy that was at the heart of both conflicts. The question posed was: would Britain be able, or willing, to maintain her vast Empire in the face of German hegemony on the continent of Europe? The answer to that question never came. Britain, in seeking to thwart German interests on the Continent, eventually lost her whole Empire in the attempt –an empire that between the wars encompassed a quarter of the earth's surface and an equal proportion of its population. Put into that context, both world wars were dangerous for Britain to fight, jeopardizing the very existence of the Empire and inevitably weakening the mother country to the point that she could not maintain her world position at the end of the conflicts.

From Germany's point of view, the wars were not only dangerous in that they finally ruined virtually every town and city, devastated the countryside and dismembered the nation; they were irrelevant. In 1890 Germany was in a position from which, within a generation, she would economically dominate the whole of Europe. Inevitably, with that economic hegemony, political hegemony would soon follow, if not even precede. By 1910 the process was well in train; had no one done anything to stop her, Germany would have achieved the Kaiser's dreams without war by the mid 1920s. The collapse of Imperial Germany in 1918, followed by temporary occupation, inflation and national humiliation, set Germany back only a few years. Despite the disasters of World War I and its aftermath, Germany was quickly recovering her old position – roughly that of 1910 – by the time Hitler took power in 1933. By 1938 German power in Europe was greater than ever before, and Britain had to face the old question once again. Could she condone German political dominance of the Continent?

In 1938 some Conservatives, like Chamberlain and Halifax, recognized the threat and were tacitly willing to maintain the Imperial status quo and condone Hitler. Other Tories, like Churchill and the Labour and Liberal Parties, wanted to challenge Germany again. Had Hitler been a bit more discreet and less hurried, perhaps a bit less flamboyant and

Below: Dunkirk, scene of an ignominious retreat by Allied forces that signaled the Fall of France.

virulently anti-Semitic, Chamberlain's policy might have succeeded. Germany would have extended her power in Europe and the Empire would have been maintained. But that was to ask the impossible, to wish that Hitler were someone other than Hitler. The result – humiliation of Britain's policy when Czechoslovakia was overrun in March 1939 – forced even Chamberlain's hand, and the stage was set for round two of the European Civil War.

World War II in Europe was very like a Greek tragedy, wherein the elements of disaster are present before the play begins, and the tragedy is writ all the larger because of the disaster's inevitability. The story of the war, told through the maps of Richard Natkiel in this volume, are signposts for the historian of human folly. In the end, Germany and Italy were destroyed, along with much of Europe. With the devastation came the inevitable collapse of both the impoverished British Empire and centuries of European hegemony in the world. A broader look from the perspective of the 1980s would indicate a further irony. Despite Germany's loss of part of its Polish and Russian territory and its division into two countries, not to mention the separation of Austria from the Reich and the semipermanent occupation of Berlin, the German economic advance was only delayed, not permanently stopped. The Federal Republic is clearly the strongest economy in Western Europe today and the fourth strongest in the world. The German Democratic Republic rates twelfth on this basis. Together their economies are roughly as strong as that of the Soviet Union, and their political reunification is now less of a dream, more of a reality toward which Germans on both sides of the Iron Curtain are striving. One day, probably within the next two decades, a form of unification may take place, and when it does, German power on the Continent will be greater than ever before. No wonder the Soviets and many Western Europeans view this prospect with fear and cynicism. What had the world wars been for? For what ideals had the blood of tens of millions been spilt?

The irony of World War II becomes even clearer when one views briefly its second half, the struggle between Japan and the United States for control of the Pacific. The question facing American Presidents from Theodore Roosevelt to Franklin Roosevelt had been: could the

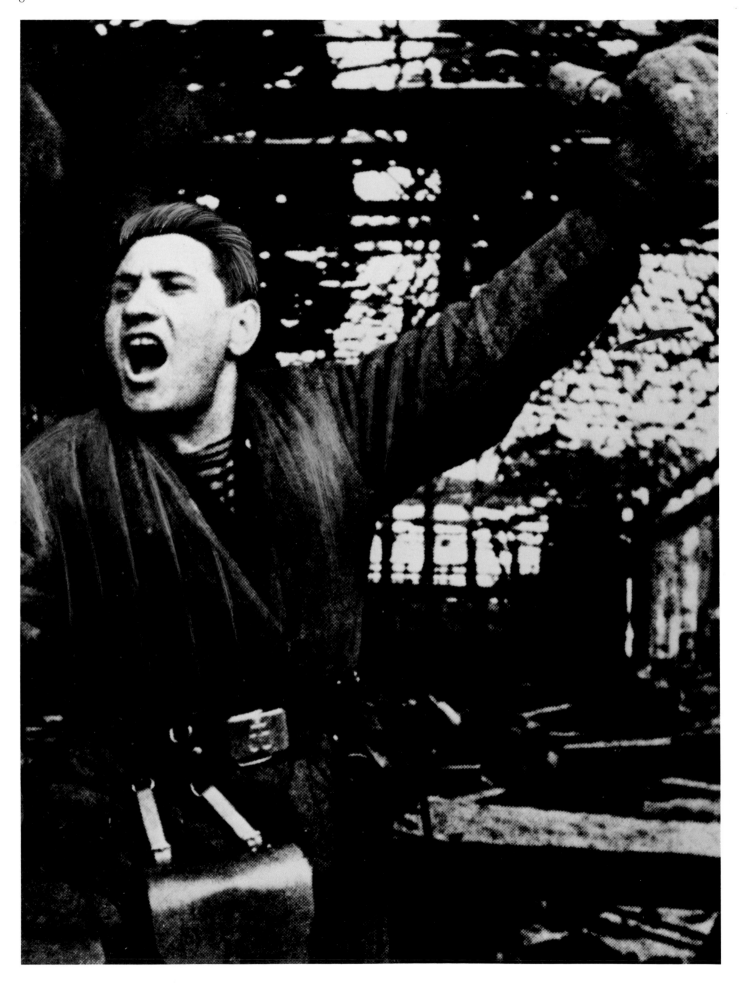

Left: The successful Russian defense of Stalingrad was a major setback to German war plans.
Below: Japanese tanks pass a wrecked British ambulance in Burma, 1942.

United States maintain its security and trade routes in the Pacific in the face of an increasingly powerful Japanese Navy and economy? For decades the question was begged, until the Japanese took matters into their own hands at Pearl Harbor, the Philippines, Vietnam and Malaya in 1941. The ensuing tragedy, as inevitable in the Pacific as was its counterpart in Europe, became obvious almost from the outset. Millions died in vain; Japan itself was devastated by fire and atomic bombs, and eventually conceded defeat.

From a forty-year perspective, what was the point of the Pacific War? Japan has the third largest economy in the world and by far the largest in Asia. In recent years the United States has actually encouraged Japan to flex its political muscles, increase its armed forces and help the United States police the Western Pacific. It would seem that this conflict was as tragically futile as the European Civil War.

The greatest disaster in the history of mankind to date was World War II. This atlas is a valuable reference work for those who feel it bears remembering. Clearly, this is the case, but the lessons of the war have been less clearly spelled out – to those who fought in it, who remember it, or who suffered from it, as well as to subsequent generations who were shaped by it and fascinated by its horrific drama. The exceptional maps of Richard Natkiel of *The Economist*, which punctuate this volume, can give only the outlines of the tragedy; they do not seek to give, nor can they give, the lessons to be learned.

It would seem that if anything useful is to be derived from studying World War II, it is this: avoid such conflicts at all costs. No nation can profit from them. This is certainly truer today than if these words had been written in 1945. The advances of science have made a future world conflict even less appetizing to those who are still mad enough to contemplate such a thing.

Perhaps the balance of the 20th century and the early years of the 21st will be very like the past 40 years: small conflicts, limited wars, brinkmanship, arms races and world tension – yes; general war, no. If our future takes this course, the period following World War II may be seen by historians of the 21st century as a time similar to the century following the Napoleonic Wars – one of growing world prosperity, which has indeed been apparent for some nations since 1945, many crises, but no all-out war. If that is our future, as it has been our recent past, the study of World War II will have been more than useful. It will have prepared the world psychologically to avoid world conflict at all cost. In that event, for the sake of a relatively stable, increasingly prosperous 'cold peace,' the 1939-45 conflict will not have been in vain. If war is the price for a bloodstained peace, those who will benefit are ourselves and future generations.

S L Mayer

Blitzkrieg

The Swastika Ascendant

The German humiliation at Versailles was skillfully exploited by Adolf Hitler and his Nazis, who rode to power in 1933 on a tide of national resentment that they had channeled to their purpose. The territorial losses, economic hardships and affronts to German pride embodied in the Treaty of Versailles virtually guaranteed the conflict that escalated into World War II. As Marshal Foch had prophesied when the treaty was forced upon a prostrate Germany: 'This is not Peace. It is an Armistice for twenty years.'

Hitler's stormy career seemed to reach its zenith when he seized control of the German Government in March of 1933. In fact, it was only beginning. Hitler im-

plemented a military build-up in defiance of the Versailles Treaty, which had limited German armed forces to an army of 100,000 and a small navy without armor or air force support. Groundwork was laid for a much larger army to be built up by conscription upon a highly trained professional base organized by General Hans von Seeckt. The prohibited tanks and planes were developed secretly, many in the Soviet Union, and future pilots were trained. Meanwhile, the Nazis continued to scapegoat the Jews and other minorities for the nation's problems; they established the first concentration camp at Dachau in the same year they came to power.

Germany withdrew from the League of

August 1939

German expansion in Europe

Nations, and by 1935 Hitler could announce repudiation of the Treaty of Versailles. He told the world that the German Air Force had been re-created, and that the army would be strengthened to 300,000 through compulsory military service. The Western democracies, France and Britain, failed to make any meaningful protest, a weakness that encouraged Hitler's ambition to restore Germany to her 'rightful place' as Europe's most powerful nation.

Nazi Germany's first overt move beyond her borders was into the Rhineland, which was reoccupied in 1936. This coup was achieved more through bravado than by superior force. Hitler's generals had counseled against it on account of the relative size of France's army, but the reoccupation was uncontested. The next step was to bring all Germans living outside the Reich into the 'Greater Germany.' Austria was annexed in March 1938, with only token protests from Britain and France. Even more ominous was Hitler's demand that Czechoslovakia turn over its western border – the Sudetenland – on ground that its three million German-speaking inhabitants were oppressed. The Nazis orchestrated a demand for annexation among the Sudeten Germans, and the Czechoslovakian Government prepared to muster its strong armed forces for resistance. Then British Prime Minister Neville Chamberlain flew to Munich to confer with Hitler.

Chamberlain rationalized that the problem was one affecting Central Europe alone, and expressed reluctance to risk war on behalf of 'a far-off country of which we know little.' France had to stand by its alliance with Britain, and the Czechoslovakian democracy was isolated in a rising sea of German expansionism. The Sudetenland, with its vital frontier defenses, was handed over. Far from securing 'peace in our time,' as Neville Chamberlain had promised after Munich, this concession opened the door to Nazi occupation of all Czechoslovakia in March 1939.

Only at this point did the Western democracies grasp the true scope of Hitler's ambitions. Belatedly, they began to rearm after years of war-weary stasis. By now Hitler's forces were more than equal to theirs, and the Führer was looking eastward, where Poland's Danzig Corridor stood between him and East Prussia, the birthplace of German militarism.

The Partition of Poland

France and Britain tried to forestall the Nazi assault on Poland by issuing a joint guarantee to the threatened nation. This was supposed to provide leverage whereby the democracies could persuade the Poles to make concessions similar to those made by the Czechs. But Hitler's aggressiveness grew more apparent throughout the spring and summer of 1939. In April he revoked both the German-Polish Non-Aggression Pact and the Anglo-German Naval Agreement of 1935. Then he sent emissaries to the Soviet Union, where Joachim von Ribbentrop concluded both an economic agreement and a Non-Aggression Pact with Josef Stalin. By 1 September 1939, the Germans were ready to invade Poland on two fronts in their first demonstration of blitzkrieg – lightning war – a strategy that combined surprise, speed and terror. It took German forces just 18 days to conquer Poland, which had no chance to complete its mobilization. The Poles had a bare dozen cavalry brigades and a few light tanks to send against nine armored divisions. A total of five German armies took part in the assault, and German superiority in artillery and infantry was at least three to one. The Polish Air Force was almost entirely destroyed on the ground by the Luftwaffe offensive supporting Army Groups North and South.

Above right: The Nazi thrust into Poland, early September.
Right: Russia counterattacks, mid to late September.
Below: The partition of Poland as agreed by Germany and Russia.

*Below: German troops enter Warsaw. The
city finally surrendered on 27 September
after 56 hours of resistance against air
and artillery attack.*

Thinly spread Polish troops staggered back from their border, and German forces were approaching Warsaw a week later. The Poles made a last-ditch effort along the Bzura River to halt the German advance against their capital, but they could not withstand the forces pitted against them. The Polish Government fled to Rumania, and on 27 September Warsaw finally capitulated.

Meanwhile, Britain and France had declared war on Germany 48 hours after the invasion of Poland. Australia, New Zealand and South Africa soon joined them. Since the Western Allies had failed in their diplomatic efforts to enlist Soviet support, they faced a united totalitarian front of Hitler's Germany and Stalin's Russia (which could be counted upon to take full advantage of Poland's impotence). Stalin had made it clear that he wanted a free hand in Eastern Europe when he cast his lot with Germany. Before the month of September was out, it became obvious that Russia and Germany had reached a secret agreement on the partition of Poland during the summer months. On 17 September Soviet troops crossed the eastern frontier to take Vilnyas; a German-Soviet Treaty of Friendship was announced two days later. On 28 September, after Warsaw's surrender, Russia annexed 77,000 square miles of eastern Poland. The other 73,000 square miles, bordering on Germany, were declared a Reich protectorate.

Blitzkrieg–North

May 1940

German expansion in Europe

Hitler counted on Allied reluctance to assume an active role in the war, and he was not disappointed. The six-month hiatus known as the Phony War lasted from September 1939 until April 1940, when Germany invaded Norway and Denmark. In the interim, Britain and France made plans that could only fail, because they were based on a negative concept: avoidance of the costly direct attacks that had characterized World War I. New Anglo-French strategy focused on naval blockade and encirclement – indirect methods that were no match for the new blitzkrieg tactics of Nazi Germany.

Early in 1940 Hitler turned his attention to Scandinavia, where he had a vested interest in Swedish iron ore imports that reached Germany via the Norwegian port of Narvik. Norway had a small Nazi Party, headed by Vidkun Quisling, that could be counted upon for fifth-column support. February brought evidence that the Allies would resist a German incursion into Norway when the *Altmark*, carrying British prisoners, was boarded in Norwegian waters by a British party. Both sides began to make plans for a Northern confrontation.

On 9 April the Germans launched their invasion of Norway and Denmark, based on a bold strategy that called for naval landings at six points in Norway, supported by waves of paratroops. The naval escort for the Narvik landing suffered heavy losses, and the defenders of Oslo sank the cruiser *Blücher* and damaged the pocket battleship *Lützow*. Even so, the Germans seized vital airfields, which allowed them to reinforce their assault units and deploy their warplanes against the Royal Navy ships along the coast.

GERMAN

SEABORNE LANDINGS AND ATTACKS
Group I PARATROOP LANDINGS
NAVAL GROUPS

ALLIES

1 Div NORWEGIAN DISPOSITIONS
LANDINGS AND ATTACKS
WITHDRAWALS

0 — MILES — 150
0 — KILOMETERS — 200

9 April
Gneisenau damaged by Renown

Narvik : 8 April
2 British destroyers sunk by German troop-ferrying destroyers.
10/13 April, 10 German destroyers sunk

✕ **8 June**
Glorious sunk, Scharnhorst damaged in naval action

9 April 1940
German forces land simultaneously at Oslo, Kristiansand, Stavanger, Bergen, Trondheim & Narvik

8 April
Hipper sinks destroyer Glowworm — Group II

18 April
Br 148 Inf Bde

10 April
Light cruiser Königsberg bombed & sunk — Group III

16 February 1940
Altmark boarded

9 April
Cruiser Karlsruhe torpedoed & sunk — Group IV

9 April 1940
German forces occupy Denmark

15 April
British, French, Polish
Br 24 Gds Bde
8 June

TROMSO
Bardufoss
HARSTAD
BJERKVIK
NARVIK 6 Div
28 May
French & Norwegian forces take Narvik
Lofoten Islands
Ofotfjord
VESTFJORDEN
Group I
15 May
30 May
BODO Saltfjord
Germans advance to relieve their force at Narvik
31 May
MO-I-RANA 14 May
MOSJOEN 10 May

NORWEGIAN SEA

16/17 April
Br 146 Inf Bde
2/3 May
NAMSOS
STEINKJER 19 Apr
Trondheim-fjord
SWEDEN
Vaernes HEGRA
TRONDHEIM 5 Div
DRAGSET 29 Apr
MOLDE
ANDALSNES
1 May ALESUND
2 May
TYNSET
30 Apr
DOMBÅS
KVAM
RENDAL 24 Apr
25 May
GUDBRANDSDALEN
OSTERDALEN
Glomma
RENA 19 Apr
ELVERUM
LILLEHAMMER 21 Apr
HAMAR
L. Mjøsa

N O R W A Y
GOL
Randsfjord
2 Div
1 May
HONEFOSS
Fornebu
9 April
Heavy cruiser Blücher sunk by shore batteries
OSLO 1 Div
KONGSBERG
4 Div
BERGEN
Oslofjord
HALDEN 12 Apr
Group V
STAVANGER
Sola
ARENDAL 27 Apr
11 April
Heavy cruiser Lützow damaged by torpedo
3 Div
KRISTIANSAND
Jösenfjord
SKAGERRAK
Group IV
KATTEGAT
AALBORG
COPENHAGEN
D E N M A R K

Denmark had already been overrun and posed no threat to German designs.

Norwegian defense forces were weak, and the Germans captured numerous arms depots at the outset, leaving hastily mobilized reservists without any weapons. Allied planning proved wholly inadequate to German professionalism and air superiority. Kristiansand, Stavanger, Bergen, Trondheim and Narvik were all lost to the Germans, along with the country's capital, Oslo. Few Allied troops were trained for landing, and those who did get ashore were poorly supplied.

In May, British, French and Polish forces attempted to recapture two important cities, but their brief success at Narvik was offset by the bungled effort at Trondheim to the south. Troops in that area had to be evacuated within two weeks, and soon after Narvik was abandoned to the Germans when events in France drew off Allied troops.

Norway and Denmark would remain under German occupation throughout the war, and it seemed that Hitler's Scandinavian triumph was complete. However, German naval losses there would hamper plans for the invasion of Britain, and the occupation would tie up numerous German troops for the duration. The Allies were not much consoled by these reflections at the time. The Northern blitzkrieg had been a heavy blow to their morale, and the Germans had gained valuable Atlantic bases for subsequent operations.

Opposite top left: The Reich expands to the north and east.
Opposite: German forces forge through Denmark and make six simultaneous landings in Norway.
Above: A Norwegian port burns as the Germans follow through their surprise attack.

Military Balance in the West

On the Western Front, both Allied and German armies scarcely stirred for six months after the declaration of war. The Allies had an ill-founded faith in their Maginot Line – still incomplete – which stretched only to the Belgian border. The threat of a German attack through Belgium, comparable to the Schlieffen Plan of 1914, was to be met through the Dyle Plan. This strategy called for blocking any advance between the Ardennes and Calais by a swift deployment of troops into Belgium from the vicinity of Sedan.

German General Erich von Manstein anticipated this plan, whose weak link was the hilly Ardennes region – widely believed to be impassable to an advancing army. Manstein prepared for an attack on the Low Countries to draw the Allies forward, followed by a swift surprise breakthrough in the Ardennes that would aim for Calais. This would cut off any Allied troops that had moved into Belgium to implement the Dyle Plan.

The Allies, discounting the possibility of a large-scale German advance through the Ardennes, garrisoned the Maginot Line and deployed their remaining forces along the Franco-Belgian border. There troops stood ready to advance to the River Dyle should the Belgians need assist-

ance. Experienced French and British units were designated for this advance, which left the sector opposite the Ardennes as the most vulnerable part of the Allied line.

On paper, the opposing forces were almost equally matched. The Allies had a total of 149 divisions as against 136 German divisions, with some 3000 armored vehicles to the Germans' 2700. But the Germans had several advantages, not the least of which was superiority in the air – some 6000 fighters and bombers to the Allies' 3300. Less tangible, but no less important, was their innovative and flexible approach to modern warfare. The Allies still clung to outmoded ideas of positional warfare, and wasted their armor in scattered deployments among their infantry divisions. The Germans massed their armor in powerful Panzer groups that could cut a swath through the most determined resistance. Where necessary, dive-bombing Stukas could support German tanks that had outstripped their artillery support in the field. It was a lethal combination.

In organization, too, the Allies lagged far behind the German war machine. Their training, communications and leadership were not comparable to those of Hitler's army, which was characterized

by dynamic co-ordination of every detail. General Maurice Gamelin, Allied Commander in Chief, now in his late sixties, was in far from vigorous health. Considerable friction developed between the British and French commands. The Allies also counted too much upon co-operation from the Belgians and the Dutch, who were slow to commit themselves for fear of provoking a German attack. German leadership, by contrast, was unified and aggressive – provided Hitler did not take a direct hand in military affairs.

Below left: Thrust and counterthrust at the Belgian border.
Bottom left: German soldiers fire at attacking aircraft from the remains of a demolished bridge, Holland, 1940.
Below: The forces of the Reich mass at the Siegfried Line.

Reserves
42 divisions

NORTH SEA

GREAT BRITAIN

NETHERLANDS

IJsselmeer

Reserves
2 divisions ■ AMSTERDAM

THE HAGUE ■
UTRECHT
ROTTERDAM ■

Dutch Army
8 divisions + res

Waal

BREDA

Maas

GERMANY

Army Group B
(Bock)
29½ divisions, inc 3 armored and 2 motorized

DOVER

OSTEND

DUNKIRK

Reserves
4 divisions

ANTWERP

Scheldt

Albert Canal

BRUSSELS ■

B E L G I U M

French Seventh Army
(Giraud)
7 divisions, inc 1 light mechanized and 2 motorized

BAILLEUL

LOUVAIN
Dyle
WAVRE

AACHEN

Supreme Commander, Armed Forces — Hitler

OKH (Army High Command)
C in C, Brauchitsch

MAULDE

NAMUR
Meuse
LIÈGE

Belgian Army
18 divisions + res

ABBEVILLE
Somme

BEF
(Gort)
9 divisions

Ardennes

Army Group A
(Rundstedt)
45½ divisions, inc 7 armored and 3 motorized

HIRSON

SEDAN

LUX.
LUXEMBOURG ■

French 1st Army Group
(Billotte)
22 divisions, inc 2 light mechanized and 3 motorized

LONGUYON

Meuse

West Wall (Siegfried Line)

Rhine

GHQ
C in C, Gamelin

Northeast Front
C in C, Georges

PARIS ■
VINCENNES

Brit

Maginot Line

HAGUENAU

Army Group C
(Leeb)
19 divisions

F R A N C E

French 2nd Army Group
(Prételat)
43 divisions + 1 British

Seine

Reserves
22 divisions, inc 3 armored

for 1st Army Group

against outflanking attack on Swiss border

General reserve

BASEL

SWITZERLAND

BERNE ■

0 ——— MILES ——— 100
0 ——— KILOMETERS ——— 160

Blitzkrieg – West

The German assault on the West was launched on 10 May 1940, when aerial bombardments and paratroop landings rained down on the Low Countries at daylight. Dutch airfields and bridges were captured, and German troops poured into Holland and Belgium. Both countries called for help from France and Britain, as the Dutch retreated from their borders, flooding their lands and demolishing strategic objectives in an attempt to halt the invasion. Their demoralization was completed by a savage air attack on Rotterdam (14 May), after which Dutch forces surrendered. Queen Wilhelmina and her government

were evacuated to England.

The French Seventh Army had tried to intervene in Holland, but it was repulsed. In Belgium, the German capture of Eben Emael, a key fortress, and the accomplishment of Manstein's plan to traverse the Ardennes with his Panzer divisions, gave access to the Meuse. Three bridgeheads were secured by 14 May, and the Allied line had been breached from Sedan to Dinant. The Panzer divisions then made for the sea, forcing back the British Expeditionary Force and two French armies in Belgium. Allied forces were split, and their attempt to link up near Arras (21 May) was a failure. German

Opposite below: German forces pour into the Low Countries.
Left: Motorized Dutch soldiers are pictured traversing a dyke.
Below: The Panzer thrust to the Meuse.

tanks had already reached the sea at Noyelles and were turning north toward the Channel ports.

Only the unwarranted caution of German commanders prevented wholesale destruction of Allied forces in Belgium. On 23 May orders to halt came down from Hitler and Field Marshal Gerd von Rundstedt. The German advance did not resume until 26 May, and the beleaguered Allies were able to fall back around Dunkirk.

Dunkirk and the Fall of France

A determined defense at Calais, and German failure to capitalize on the chance of seizing the Channel ports, enabled the Royal Navy to begin evacuating British troops from Dunkirk. Between 27 May, when Allied resistance at Calais ended, and 4 June, 338,226 men of the British Expeditionary Force left Dunkirk along with 120,000 French soldiers. The Germans tried to prevent the rescue operation with attacks by the Luftwaffe, but the Royal Air Force distinguished itself in safeguarding the exodus. With the loss of only 29 planes, RAF pilots accounted for 179 German aircraft in the four-day period beginning 27 May. Royal Navy losses totaled six destroyers sunk and 19 badly damaged, plus many smaller craft. The toll in lives and matériel would have been much higher had chance not favored the Allies in the form of Germany's inexplicable pause at Noyelles.

To the south, General Maxime Weygand tried to rally remaining French forces for defense of the Somme Line. The Germans began to attack south on 5 June, and the line gave way despite courageous fighting by many French units. By 10 June the Germans had crossed

the Seine, and Mussolini took advantage of the situation by declaring war on France. Italian troops moved in and encountered stiff resistance, but overall French morale and confidence were at a low ebb. The government removed to Bordeaux and rejected Prime Minister Winston Churchill's offer of a union between Britain and France. By 16 June Premier Reynaud was resigning in favor of Marshal Henri Pétain, who announced the next day that France was seeking an armistice.

The conquered nation was divided into occupied and unoccupied zones. The Pétain Government would rule the unoccupied zone from Vichy and collaborate closely with the Germans, to the revulsion of most Frenchmen. The 'Free French,' led by Charles de Gaulle, a young army officer and politician, repudiated the Vichy régime and departed for England, where de Gaulle announced that France would ultimately throw off the German oppressors.

June 1940

German expansion in Europe

Above: Germany expands westwards to the Channel coast.
Below: The Allied front line contracts as France and Belgium are overrun.

Far left: The Allies prepare to evacuate as the Germans advance.
Left: France divided under Nazi and Vichy rule.
Below: The occupying forces move into Paris in June.

24

Left: German vacillation and the spirited defense of Calais gave the Allies time to evacuate from Dunkirk.
Below: A British soldier is hit by strafing Luftwaffe aircraft on the Dunkirk beach.
Bottom: The British Expeditionary Force and their French allies await departure.
Right: The aftermath of evacuation.
Below right: The German sweep southwards through France that resulted in the 22 June armistice. Note Italian incursions from the southeast.

GREAT BRITAIN

DOVER

BELGIUM

Army Group B

Pz Group Kleist

Army Group A

Hoth's
XV Pz
Corps

XIV Pz
Corps

XVI Pz
Corps

Second and
Ninth Armies

GERMANY

ENGLISH CHANNEL

Somme

Rhine

Pz Group Guderian

9 June

Army Group C

ABBEVILLE

ST VALÉRY
FÉCAMP

CHERBOURG
18 June

Channel
Islands

DIEPPE

AMIENS

PERONNE

Fr Seventh
Army

SEDAN

LUX.

XXXIX Pz
Corps

XLI Pz Corps

LE HAVRE

Fr Tenth Army

ROUEN

RETHEL

Fr Second
Army

VERDUN

Maginot Line

CAEN

COMPIÈGNE

Oise

Fr Sixth
Army

RHEIMS

Fr Fourth
Army

METZ

STRASBOURG

BREST 19 June

PARIS
14 June

CHALONS

NANCY

ALENÇON

CHARTRES

Seine

ST DIZIER

Marne

Meuse

EPINAL

22 June
Trapped French Third,
Fifth & Eighth Armies
surrender

RENNES

LE MANS

ORLÉANS

TROYES

BELFORT

BASLE

ANGERS

TOURS

Loire

Cher

BRIARE 18 June

DIJON
16 June

SWITZERLAND

NANTES
19 June

SAUMUR
19 June

VIERZON

NEVERS

PONTARLIER
17 June

BERNE

FRANCE

POITIERS

Saône

BAY OF BISCAY

ROYAN
25 June

ANGOULÊME

LIMOGES

VICHY
20 June

GENEVA

ITALY

22 June 1940
Line reached by German
forces at armistice

CLERMONT
FERRAND

ST ETIENNE

LYONS
20 June

LANSLEBOURG

TURIN

BORDEAUX

Garonne

Rhône

GRENOBLE

BRIANÇON

Italy declares
war 10 June 1940,
attacks 21 June

TOULOUSE

ST JEAN DE LUZ
27 June

NICE

MENTON

MARSEILLES

TOULON

GERMAN CONTROLLED, 4 JUNE, 1940

WEYGAND LINE, 4 JUNE

FRONT LINE, 11/12 JUNE

SPAIN

PERPIGNAN

MEDITERRANEAN SEA

0   MILES   150

0   KILOMETERS   250

The Attack on Britain

Right: The stage is set for the Battle of Britain, 1940.
Below: London's dockland burns after one of the first major bombing raids on the capital, 7 September 1940.

The Battle of Britain was fought in the air to prevent a seaborne invasion of the British Isles. The German invasion plan, code-named Operation Sealion, took shape when Britain failed to sue for peace, as Hitler had expected, after the fall of France. On 16 July 1940, German Armed Forces were advised that the Luftwaffe must defeat the RAF, so that Royal Navy ships would be unprotected if they tried to prevent a cross-Channel invasion. It was an ambitious project for the relatively small German Navy, but success would hinge upon air power, not sea power.

There were only some 25 divisions on British home ground, widely scattered and ill supplied with equipment and transport. The RAF alone could gain the time necessary for the army to re-equip after Dunkirk, and hold off the Germans until stormy fall weather made it impossible to launch Operation Sealion. The air arm was well led by Air Chief Marshal Hugh Dowding, who made the most of his relatively small but skillful force. The RAF had the advantage of a good radar system, which the Germans unwisely neglected to destroy, and profited also from the German High Command's decision to concentrate on the cities rather than airfields.

All-out Luftwaffe attacks did not begin until 13 August, which gave Britain time to make good some of the losses incurred at Dunkirk and to train additional pilots. On 7 September London became the main German target, relieving pressure on British airfields which had suffered in earlier bombings. RAF pilots who were shot down unwounded could, and often did, return to combat on the same day, while German pilots were captured. The short-range Messerschmitt Bf 109 could stay over England only briefly if it were

RAF FIGHTER COMMAND

- (HQ) COMMAND HEADQUARTERS
- (G) GROUP HEADQUARTERS
- ○ SECTOR STATION & BOUNDARY*
- ● FIGHTER STATION
- + LOW-LEVEL RADAR STATION
- ⊕ HIGH-LEVEL RADAR STATION
- – – – COMMAND BOUNDARY
- 🔥 TOWNS BOMBED

LUFTWAFFE BASES

- ⊕ BOMBER
- ● STUKA (DIVE-BOMBER)
- • FIGHTER (Bf 109)
- ⊙ TWIN-ENGINED FIGHTER (Bf110)
- – – – COMMAND BOUNDARY

MILES 0 ———— 100

KILOMETRES 0 ———— 150

*11 Group only

GLASGOW

BELFAST

FIRTH OF FORTH

NEWCASTLE

(G) SUNDERLAND

Fighter Command 13 Group (Saul)

MIDDLESBROUGH

Luftflotte 5 (Stumpff)
(from Norway and Denmark)

N O R T H   S E A

Cover of low-level radar (500 ft)

Cover of high-level radar (15,000 ft)

LIVERPOOL

MANCHESTER

SHEFFIELD

HULL

(G) NOTTINGHAM

Fighter Command 12 Group (Leigh-Mallory)

BIRMINGHAM

COVENTRY

NORWICH

Duxford

IPSWICH   Martlesham

Debden

ROTTERDAM

SWANSEA

CARDIFF

BRISTOL   Ball

BATH

Andover

Middle Wallop

SOUTHAMPTON

Fighter Command 10 Group (Brand)

Stanmore
Northolt

Uxbridge (G)

(HQ)   LOND

North Weald

Rochford

Hornchurch

Croydon

Biggin Hill

Kenley

Redhill

West Malling

Detling

THAMES ESTUARY

Eastchurch   Manston

CANTERBURY

Lympne   Hawkinge

Fighter Command 11 Group (Park)

Tangmere

PORTSMOUTH

VENTNOR

EXETER

PLYMOUTH

E N G L I S H   C H A N N E L

CALAIS

GHENT

ANTWERP

B E L G I U M

LILLE

Luftflotte 2 (Kesselring)

AMIENS

CHERBOURG

LE HAVRE

F R A N C E

PARIS

Luftflotte 3 (Sperrle)

RENNES

Bottom: Two Luftwaffe Dornier Do 17 bombers over the River Thames, September 1940.
Right: Aftermath of heavy night bombing in the Midlands city of Coventry two months later.

to return to its base in France, which helped cancel out the German superiority in numbers of planes and pilots.

The Battle of Britain raged in the skies for almost two months, while a German fleet of barges and steamers awaited the signal to depart the Channel ports for the British coast. By mid September, the invasion date had already been put off three times, and Hitler had to concede that the Luftwaffe had failed in its mission. Sporadic German bombing would continue until well into 1941, but Operation Sealion was 'postponed' indefinitely.

The Invasion of Yugoslavia

On 6 April 1941, the Germans moved to extend their influence in the Balkans by an attack on Yugoslavia, whose Regent, Prince Paul, had been coerced into signing the Tripartite Pact on 25 March. As a result, he was deposed by a Serbian coalition that placed King Peter on the throne in a government that would last only a matter of days. Hitler ordered 33 divisions into Yugoslavia, and heavy air raids struck Belgrade in a new display of blitzkrieg. At the same time, the Yugoslav Air Force was knocked out before it could come to the nation's defense.

The German plan called for an incursion from Bulgaria by the Twelfth Army, which would aim south toward Skopje and Monastir to prevent Greek assistance to the Yugoslavs. Thence they would move into Greece itself, for the invasion that had been planned since the previous year. Two days later, General Paul von Kleist would lead his First Panzer Group toward Nis and Belgrade, where it would be joined by the Second Army and other units that included Italians, Hungarians and Germans.

The plan worked smoothly, and there was little resistance to any of the attacks mounted between 6 and 17 April, when an armistice was agreed after King Peter left the country. Internal dissension among the various Yugoslavian states was a help to the Germans, who lost fewer than 200 men in the entire campaign. Another factor in their favor was the defenders' use of an ineffectual cordon deployment that was no match for the strength and numbers thrown against them. German air superiority completed the case against Yugoslavian autonomy.

Below: Yugoslavia falls in the face of pressure from Germany, Hungary and Italy, April 1941.

The states of Yugoslavia

The Battle for Greece

Below: Italian attacks and Greek counteroffensives, winter 1940-41. Right: The British evacuate the Greek mainland as Axis forces thrust southwards.

The overthrow of Yugoslavia's Regency Government on 27 March 1941 changed Hitler's scenario for southeastern Europe. Prior to that, he had planned to assist his Italian allies in their ill-starred Greek campaign by persuading Bulgaria and Yugoslavia to allow his troops free passage into Greece. Now he would have to invade both Yugoslavia and Greece, where the British were landing over 50,000 men in an attempt to enforce their 1939 guarantee of Greek independence.

Mussolini's forces had crossed the Greek frontier into Albania on 28 October 1940, but their fortunes had been going downhill since November. The Greeks mobilized rapidly and pushed the Italians back until half of Albania was recovered, with British assistance, by March of 1941. The prospect of his ally's defeat, coupled with British proximity to the oil fields of Rumania, motivated Hitler to send three full army corps, with a strong armor component, into Greece. The attack was launched on 6 April, simultaneously with the invasion of Yugoslavia.

Allied forces in Greece included seven Greek divisions – none of them strong – less than two divisions from Australia and New Zealand, and a British armored brigade, as well as the forces deployed in Albania. British leaders wanted to base their defense on the Aliakmon Line, where topography favored them, with sufficient forces to close the Monastir Gap. But the Greek Commander in Chief held out for a futile attempt to protect Greek Macedonia, which drew off much-needed troops to the less-defensible Metaxas Line. The Germans seized their chance to destroy this line in direct attacks and push other troops through the Monastir Gap to outflank the Allied defense lines.

By 10 April the German offensive was in high gear and rolling over the Aliakmon Line, which had to be evacuated. A week later, General Archibald Wavell declined to send any more British reinforcements from Egypt – a sure sign that the fight for Greece was being abandoned. Some 43,000 men were evacuated to Crete before the Germans closed the last Peloponnesian port at Kalamata; 11,000 others were left behind.

Right: German mountain infantry march through the township of Lamia in April 1941.

■ SOFIA

YUGOSLAVIA

KYUSTENDIL

Twelfth Army
(List)

KRIVA PALANKA

XL Pz Corps

PLOVDIV   *Maritza*

DELČEVO

■ SHKODËR

SKOPJE
8 Apr

KOCANI

B U L G A R I A

Vardar

VELES
6 Apr

STRUMICA

Struma

NEVROKOP

XVIII Corps

XXX Corps

ALBANIA

■ TIRANË

PRILEP

Beles Mts

Rupel Pass

Nestos

EKHÍNOS

XANTHI

Thrace

KOMOTINÍ

DURRES

ELBASAN

Shkumbin

L Okhrida

MONASTIR
9 Apr

Prespa

Monastir
Gap

DOJRAN

SERRAI

DRAMA

KAVALLA

**Gr Second
Army**

ALEXANDROÚPOLIS

**Ital Ninth
Army**

FLÓRINA

L Vegorritis

EDHESSA

Axios

KILKIS

THESSALONIKI
9 Apr

M a c e d o n i a

THASOS
16 Apr

SAMOTHRACE
19 Apr

**Ital Eleventh
Army**

VALONA

KORCE

AMINDAION

*Vermion
Mts*

VEROIA

KLISSOURA

PTOLEMAÏS

M

TEPELENE

Vijose

KOZÁNI

Aliakmon

Piéria Óri

KATERINI

LÍMNOS

23 April

Venetikos

SERVIA
16 April

▲ *Mt Olympus*

GJIROKASTER

SARANDË

P
I
N
D
U
S

M
O
U
N
T
A
I
N
S

**Gr First
Army**

'W' Force
(Wilson)

▲ *Mt Ossa*

LÍMNOS

CORFU

IOÁNNINA
20 Apr

LÁRISA
19 Apr

Surrenders
23 April

PARAMITHIA

TRIKKALA

Pinios

*PLAIN OF
THESSALY*

VOLOS

Æ G E A N

SKÍROS

LESBOS
4 May

ÁRTA

G R E E C E

LEVKAS

LAMIA

Thermopylai
BRÁLLOS

MOLOS

Evvoia
(Eubœa)

S E A

KHÍOS
4 May

KEFALLINÍA

20 April

MESOLÓNGION
26 Apr

Akhelóos

Gulf of Corinth

THEBES

I O N I A N

ZÁKINTHOS

PÁTRAI

ATHENS
27 Apr

RÁFINA

ÁNDROS

S E A

PÍRGOS

CORINTH
26 Apr

PIRAEUS

PORTO RÁFTI

TÍNOS

Peloponnesos

TRÍPOLIS

NÁUPLIA

ZÁKINTHOS

KALAMATA
28 Apr

MONEMVASÍA

MÍLOS

NÁXOΣ

C Matapan

KÍTHIRA

British evacuation
routes

*Suda
Bay*

CANEA

HERÁKLION

CRETE

| STABILISED FRONT IN ALBANIA, 6 APRIL 1941 |
| METAXAS LINE |
| ALIAKMON LINE |
| THE FRONT AT DATES SHOWN |
| GERMAN AIRBORNE LANDING, 26 APRIL |
| HEIGHT IN FEET |

	OVER 6000
	3000–6000
	1200–3000
	UNDER 1200

0   MILES   100

0   KILOMETERS   160

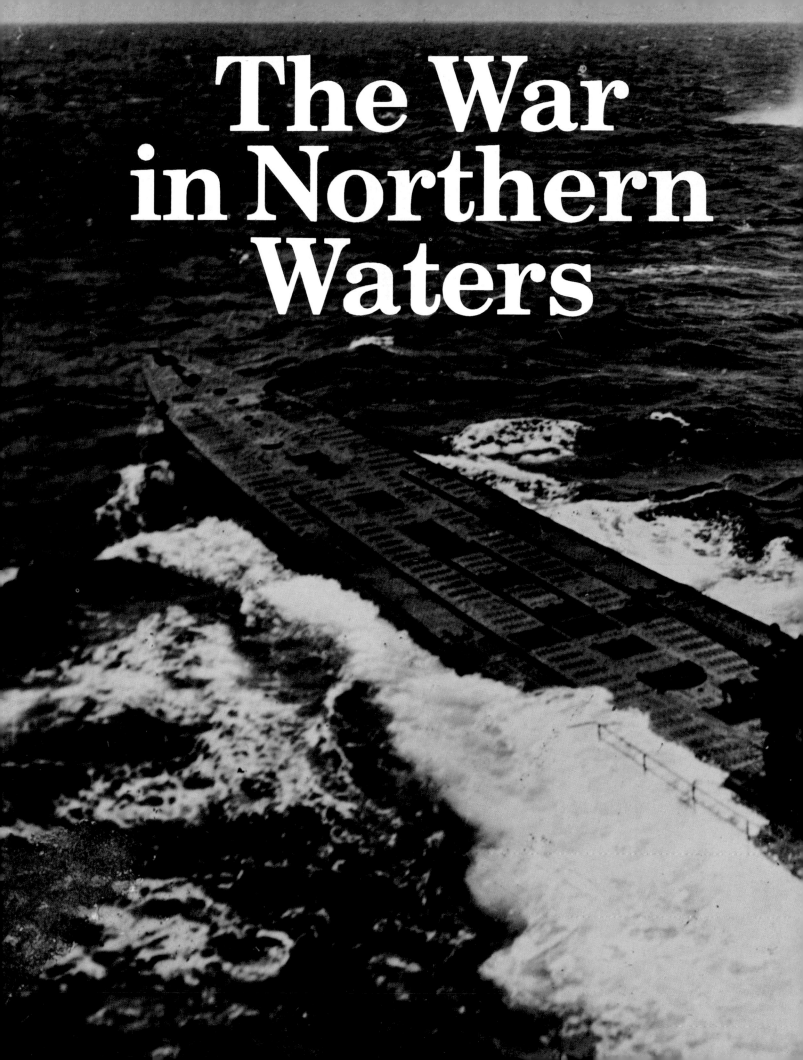

The War
in Northern
Waters

Battle of the Atlantic 1939-42

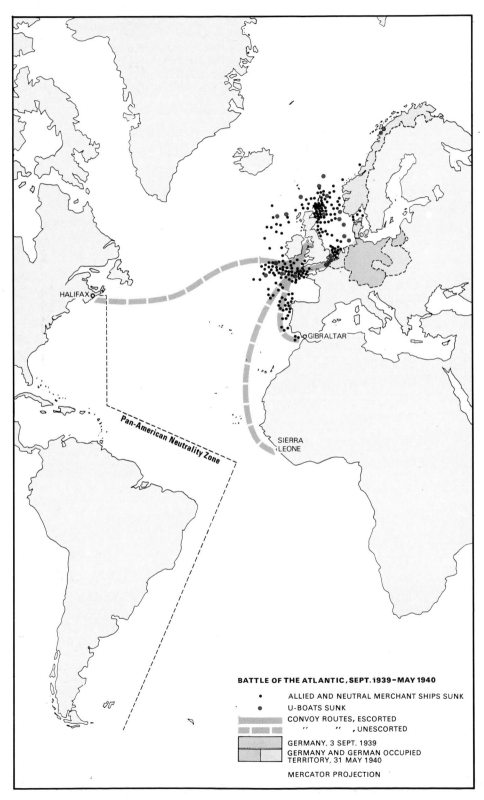

BATTLE OF THE ATLANTIC, SEPT. 1939—MAY 1940

- •   ALLIED AND NEUTRAL MERCHANT SHIPS SUNK
- ●   U-BOATS SUNK

CONVOY ROUTES, ESCORTED

     "   " , UNESCORTED

GERMANY, 3 SEPT. 1939

GERMANY AND GERMAN OCCUPIED TERRITORY, 31 MAY 1940

MERCATOR PROJECTION

The memory of German submarine success in World War I led the British to introduce a convoy system as soon as hostilities began. The immediate threat was less than British leaders imagined, because submarine construction had not been given high priority in the German rearmament program, and Hitler was reluctant to antagonize neutral nations by unrestricted submarine warfare. This was fortunate for the British in the early months of the war, because they lacked sufficient escort vessels. Many ships sailed independently, and others were convoyed only partway on their voyages.

In June 1940 the U-boat threat became more pressing. The fall of France entailed the loss of support from the French Fleet even as British naval responsibility increased with Italian participation in the war. Germany's position was strengthened by the acquisition of bases in western France and Norway for their long-range reconnaissance support planes

Previous pages: A surfaced German U-boat immediately prior to its sinking by US Navy bombers southwest of Ascension Island, November 1943.
Opposite and below right: Early developments in the Battle of the Atlantic.
Below: USS Spencer closes on a U-boat off the east coast of America.

and U-boats. And German submarines, if relatively few in number, had several technical advantages. Their intelligence was superior to that of the British due to effective code-breaking by the German signals service. British Asdic equipment could detect only submerged submarines; those on the surface were easily overlooked at night or until they approached within striking distance of a convoy. Radar was not sophisticated, and British patrol aircraft were in very short supply.

As a result, the Battle of the Atlantic was not one of ships alone. It involved technology, tactics, intelligence, air power and industrial competition. The Germans made full use of their advantages in the second half of 1940 (known to German submariners as 'the happy time'). U-boat 'wolf-packs' made concerted attacks on convoys to swamp their escorts, and numerous commanders won renown for the speed and success of their missions.

BATTLE OF THE ATLANTIC, JUNE 1940 – MARCH 1941

- •   ALLIED AND NEUTRAL MERCHANT SHIPS SUNK
- ●   U-BOATS SUNK
-      CONVOY ROUTES, ESCORTED
-      "   "   , UNESCORTED
-      AXIS AND AXIS OCCUPIED TERRITORY, 31 MAR. 1941

MERCATOR PROJECTION

HALIFAX
GIBRALTAR
SIERRA LEONE
Pan-American Neutrality Zone

BATTLE OF THE ATLANTIC, APRIL 1941–DEC. 1941

•	ALLIED AND NEUTRAL MERCHANT SHIPS SUNK
•	U-BOATS SUNK
■	U BOAT SUPPLY SHIPS SUNK
	CONVOY ROUTES
	ALLIED AIR COVER ZONES
	AXIS AND AXIS OCCUPIED TERRITORY, 31 DEC. 1941
	MERCATOR PROJECTION

By March 1941 this picture was changing. Many U-boats had been destroyed, and replacement construction was not keeping pace. The British provided stronger escorts and made use of rapidly developing radar capabilities to frustrate German plans. Three of the best German U-boat commanders were killed that March, and Churchill formed the effective Battle of the Atlantic Committee to co-ordinate British efforts in every sphere of the struggle. The remainder of 1941 proved that a balance had been struck: German U-boats tripled in number between March and November, but shipping losses in November were the lowest of the war to that date. US assistance in both convoy duty and supplies helped improve the British position, as did intelligence breakthroughs.

When the United States formally en-

Opposite and below right: The Battle of the Atlantic continues, with Allied air cover now apparent.
Below: US troops disembark in Iceland. Air cover from Reykjavik drastically reduced U-boat strikes in the area from 1941 onwards.

tered the war at the end of 1941, the situation changed again. The US Navy was preoccupied with the Japanese threat in the Pacific, and the East Coast was left vulnerable to German submarine operations. For the first half of 1942, the US ships sailed without escorts, showed lights at night and communicated without codes – afflicted by the same peacetime mentality that had proved so disastrous at Pearl Harbor. Sparse anti-submarine patrols along the East Coast were easily evaded by the experienced Germans. It was months before an effective convoy system was established and extended as far south as the Caribbean. But by late summer of 1942 the US coastline was no longer a happy hunting ground, and the U-boats turned their attention back to the main North Atlantic routes.

BATTLE OF THE ATLANTIC, JAN.1942–JULY 1942

- ALLIED AND NEUTRAL MERCHANT SHIPS SUNK
- U-BOATS SUNK
- CONVOY ROUTES
- ALLIED AIR COVER ZONES
- AXIS AND AXIS OCCUPIED TERRITORY, 31 JULY 1942

MERCATOR PROJECTION

Stalking the *Bismarck*

The formidable German battleship *Bismarck* was ready for action in the spring of 1941. Armed with 15-inch guns and protected by massive armor plate, she was an ocean raider to reckon with, accompanied on her first foray by the heavy cruiser *Prinz Eugen*, which had finished her trials at the same time. On 18 May the two warships left Gdynia for Bergen, where RAF reconnaissance planes spotted them two days later. Their presence in Norwegian waters could only mean a foray into the Atlantic, and Royal Navy vessels in and around Britain were warned of the coming confrontation. Meanwhile, the German ships put to sea in foggy weather, bound for the Denmark Strait under command of Vice-Admiral Günther Lütjens. Not until late on 23 May were they spotted in the Strait by the cruisers *Suffolk* and *Norfolk*.

British Vice-Admiral Lancelot Holland, commanding the *Hood* and the new battleship *Prince of Wales*, altered course to intercept the raiders. *Prince of Wales* still had workmen aboard and was by no means fully prepared to fight. *Hood* was a veteran, but she took a German shell in one of her aft magazines just as she closed with *Bismarck* and blew up. Only three crew members of 1500 survived. *Bismarck* then scored several direct hits on *Prince of Wales*, ending the engagement. Leaking fuel from a ruptured tank, *Bismarck* left the scene, shadowed by *Prince of Wales* and two cruisers. *Prinz Eugen* broke away and returned to Brest, and the Royal Navy lost contact with the damaged German battleship. On 26 May she was spotted by an RAF Catalina north of Gibraltar.

Force H, heading northeast from Gibraltar, included the carrier *Ark Royal*, which launched her Swordfish against the disabled *Bismarck*. A torpedo strike jammed *Bismarck*'s rudder and left her an easy prey to the battleships *Rodney* and *King George V*, which arrived that night (26-27 May) to pour heavy-caliber shells into the German warship. A torpedo from the cruiser *Dorsetshire* completed the *Bismarck*'s destruction. She sank with all but 110 men of her crew, which numbered 2300.

Below: Charting the Bismarck's *course to destruction, May 1941.*
Right: The loss of Allied convoy PQ-17 in July 1942 proved a grievous blow to morale. Almost two-thirds of the ships involved failed to reach their destination, Archangel, and thousands of tons of urgently needed matériel were lost.

The Arctic Convoys

MERCHANT SHIPS SUNK BY U-BOATS AND BOMBERS

MERCHANT SHIP RUN AGROUND

GERMAN AIR BASES

0   NAUTICAL MILES   200

SPITZBERGEN

Ayrshire escorts Silver Sword, Troubadour and Ironclad through ice barrier to Novaya Zemlya and Archangel

Bolton Castle   Washington

Paulus Potter

HOPE I

2215 PQ-17 scatters

Earlston   Pankraft

2215 4 July PQ-17 scatters

Empire Byron   River Afton

Carlton

Cruiser and destroyer escort head South

Aldersdale   Daniel Morgan

ROUTE OF PQ-17

Honomu   Zaafaran

BEAR ISLAND

Fairfield City

Peter Kerr

Sunk 5 July

B A R E N T S   S E A

Matochkin Strait

Zemlya

Hartlebury

Pan Atlantic

Sunk 6/8 July

Winston Salem

Olopana

John Witherspoon

Novaya

Alcoa Ranger

Afternoon, 5 July
Tirpitz, Scheer, Hipper and 6 destroyers sail

2130, 5 July
Operation abandoned due to success of attacks by German bombers and submarines on PQ-17

North Cape

Alten Fjord

LOFOTEN ISLANDS

TROMSO

BANAK

KOLGUEV I

Hoosier

BARDUFOSS

KIRKENES

El Capitan   Sunk 10 July

NARVIK

NORWAY

PETSAMO

Cape Kanin

SWEDEN

FINLAND

MURMANSK

RUSSIA

IOKANGA

To White Sea & Archangel

Hazardous duty fell to the men who convoyed supplies to Russia after the German invasion of June 1941. The forces of nature on the arctic run posed a threat equal to that of the Germans. Savage storms and shifting ice packs were a constant menace. In the summer months, the pack ice retreated north, and convoys could give a wider berth to enemy airfields on the Norwegian and Finnish coasts, but the long summer daylight made them vulnerable to U-boats. When the ice edge moved south again, the U-boat threat lessened with the hours of daylight, but it was more difficult to stand clear of the airfields.

Many Allied seamen lost their lives on the arctic run, including most of the members of PQ-17, which sailed for Russia on 27 June 1942. Thirty-six merchant ships were heavily escorted by Allied destroyers, battleships, submarines, a carrier and various smaller craft. Near Bear Island in the Barents Sea, the convoy lost its shadowing aircraft in heavy fog. At the same time, word came that German surface ships *Tirpitz*, *Scheer* and *Hipper* had left their southern bases.

Early on 4 July, German planes torpedoed a merchantman and sank two ships of the convoy. The German ships arrived at Altenfjord, Norway, and operations control in London expected an imminent sailing to intercept the convoy, whose distant cover had been withdrawn per previous plans. Sir Dudley Pound, First Sea Lord, saw a chance for the convoy's ships to evade the German raiders by scattering; orders to this effect were issued on 4 July. The long-range escort, except for the submarines, left the convoy to rendez-

vous with the close cover, leaving PQ-17 scattered and defenseless. German U-boats and aircraft began to pick off the hapless ships, and the surface-ship mission that set sail from Altenfjord on 5 July was canceled as unnecessary late that day.

Between 5 and 8 July, almost two-thirds of the convoy was sunk in icy waters hundreds of miles from its destination of Archangel. The armed trawler *Ayrshire* succeeded in leading three merchantmen up into the ice, where they camouflaged themselves with white paint and rode out the crisis. These three were among the eleven merchant ships that finally reached Russia with desperately needed supplies. The other 25 went down with their crews and thousands of tons of matériel destined for the Soviet war effort.

The Sea Roads Secured, 1943-45

BATTLE OF THE ATLANTIC, AUG. 1942–MAY 1943

- · ALLIED AND NEUTRAL MERCHANT SHIPS SUNK
- • U-BOATS SUNK
- ▬ CONVOY ROUTES
- ⌒ ALLIED AIR COVER ZONES
- ▢ AXIS AND AXIS OCCUPIED TERRITORY, 31 MAY 1943

MERCATOR PROJECTION

By mid 1942 the Battle of the Atlantic had shifted away from the US East Coast to more distant areas, where German U-boats continued to make successful raids on Allied shipping. Many oil tankers and other vessels were lost south of the Caribbean, off the Brazilian coast and around the Cape of Good Hope. Before the year was out, the Allies had augmented the convoy system by specially trained Support Groups – escort vessels that would help endangered convoys or seek out U-boats in areas where they had been detected. These groups usually included a small aircraft carrier and an escort carrier, along with surface forces. They were free of normal escort duties and could therefore hunt the U-boats to destruction.

A cryptographic breakthrough at the end of 1942 increased Allied intelligence on German deployments, and changes in the code system (June 1943) made it more difficult for the Germans to anticipate Allied movements. Even so, late 1942 and early 1943 brought great difficulties. Allied commitments were increased by the invasion of North Africa, which drew off North Atlantic escort forces, with

Opposite: Continuation and (below right) conclusion of the Battle of the Atlantic. Below: A U-boat victim burns in mid-Atlantic. By the summer of 1943 the worst Allied shipping losses were over.

corresponding shipping losses. In March 1943, the climax of the Battle of the Atlantic, 120 Allied ships were sunk. Then the support groups returned from North African waters, and the US industrial effort paid dividends in accelerated production of escort carriers and other needed equipment. Improvements in radar and long-range scout planes, years in the making, came to the fore, and Allied crews began to capitalize on their hard-won experience. In April 1943, shipping losses declined, and the following month 41 U-boats were destroyed. On 22 May the German submarines were ordered to withdraw from the North Atlantic.

After the summer of 1943, the U-boats were never again the threat that they had been. The 'wolf-pack' tactic was abandoned in 1944, and the remaining submarines prowled singly in an area increasingly focused around the British Isles. At the war's end, fewer than 200 were still operational. Allied victory in the Atlantic was largely a function of superior co-ordination of effort, which ultimately offset the initial German advantage in submarine technology.

BATTLE OF THE ATLANTIC, JUNE 1943–MAY 1945

- • ALLIED AND NEUTRAL MERCHANT SHIPS SUNK
- • U-BOATS SUNK
- CONVOY ROUTES
- ALLIED AIR COVER ZONES
- AXIS AND AXIS OCCUPIED TERRITORY, 31 MAY 1944 / 7 MAY 1945

MERCATOR PROJECTION

The Desert War and the Mediterranean

Rommel's First Offensive

Previous pages: The German retreat from El Alamein, November 1942.
Right: The Germans press eastwards through Libya into Egypt.
Below: Rommel enters Egypt.
Bottom left: Rommel and his officers inspect a captured British tank.
Bottom: The Allies isolated at Tobruk.
Below right: Rommel directs operations.

The first German troops began landing in North Africa on February 1941, under command of General Erwin Rommel, who would earn the nickname 'Desert Fox.' His leadership abilities were acknowledged by comrades and enemies alike. Rommel soon saw that British forces in Africa were weak, and that no reinforcements would be forthcoming. On 24 March German forces took El Agheila easily, and the 5 Light Division went on to attack the British 2 Armored Division at Mersa Brega. There they encountered stiff resistance, but the British failed to counterattack and lost their advantage.

Instead of choosing among three alternative courses of attack, Rommel moved boldly on all three fronts: north to Benghazi, northeast to Msus and Mechili and east to Tengeder, to threaten British supply lines. Field Marshal Archibald Wavell, in overall command of British forces, lacked the men to counter this multiple attack, launched on 5 April. His single armored division fell back and was reduced to a remnant by mechanical failure. The defense at Mechili, 3 Indian Brigade, was soon overwhelmed, with what remained of the 2 Armored Division. The 8 Australian Division retreated from Benghazi to Derna, thence toward Tobruk, which was being reinforced with the 7 Australian Division.

On 14 April the German 5 Light Division penetrated the Tobruk perimeter a short distance, but was driven back. Italian troops were now coming up to replace the German units making ready to cross the Egyptian frontier. The British garrison at Tobruk was isolated in the midst of Axis forces, and on 25 April the Germans broke through the Halfaya Pass into Egypt. Rommel was dissatisfied with the failure to capture Tobruk, and another full-scale attack struck the British there on 30 April. Axis troops pushed a salient into the western sector, but it was contained after four days of fighting.

The German Drive on Gazala

Rommel's German units, the *Deutsches Afrika Korps* (DAK), and their allies suffered a setback in the Crusader Battles with the British Eighth Army late in 1941. Tobruk was relieved, and Rommel had to pull back to El Agheila, having suffered 38,000 Axis casualties as against 18,000 for the British. His men were exhausted, supplies were running out and 300 German tanks had been destroyed in the Libyan desert.

British forces pursued Rommel to El Agheila, believing that his shattered units would be unable to react. However, successful air raids on Malta had restored the German supply line across the Mediterranean, and Rommel's forces were quickly rebuilt to fighting strength. On 21 January 1942 they made an unexpected advance that pushed Eighth Army back toward Agedabia. In a matter of days the British faced encirclement at Benghazi and were forced to retreat to the defensive position at Gazala. The line there consisted of minefields running south to Bir Hacheim and a series of fortified keeps that were manned by XIII Corps brigades.

DAK forces under Cruewell swung around Bir Hacheim on 26 May to outflank the Gazala Line, but they were attacked from both sides on Sidra Ridge and stopped short with loss of a third of their armor. Their water and fuel were running out, and Rommel tried to push a supply line through the British minefields without success. He then moved all his remaining armor into 'the Cauldron' to await the impending British counterattack.

Cruewell's isolated forces were finally supplied on 4 June, and Eighth Army failed to counterattack until 5/6 June, when it was beaten off with heavy losses. The defense at Bir Hacheim crumbled and DAK broke out of the Cauldron to force the British back from the Gazala Line even beyond Tobruk. Axis forces had surrounded the British garrison there by 18 June.

Opposite above: Rommel advances eastwards, pushing the Eighth Army back toward Gazala and Tobruk.

Opposite: The Allied stand on 26 May, with fortified keeps (shaded) scattered along the minefield (bold line).

Above left: Breakout from the Cauldron. Below: An Afrika Korps Panzer III advances.

The Fall of Tobruk

Eighth Army was severely demoralized by the German triumph at Gazala, which contributed to the distrust between infantry and tank units that had surfaced during the Crusader Battles. British leadership had failed to capitalize on several advantages, including a numerical superiority in armor, the DAK containment in the Cauldron and the well-prepared defense line at Gazala.

Rommel launched his drive on Tobruk from the southeastern sector on 20 June 1942. Heavy dive-bomber attacks displayed German air superiority to devastating effect, after which DAK pushed through the perimeter defenses. By midmorning German troops had reached the minefields, and the airfields were overrun soon after. At 1900 hours 21 Panzer Division moved into Tobruk.

There was sporadic fighting within the perimeter through the night, but the Germans had overcome almost all resistance by the morning of 21 June. General Klopper, the South African in command of the garrison, surrendered, and the road to Egypt was open.

Right: The perimeter defenses are breached, and the fall of Tobruk is less than 12 hours away.
Below: British troops surrender to their Axis adversaries. Rommel's victory, completed on 21 June, cleared the way for an advance into Egypt.

The Naval War in the Mediterranean

The map at the top:

2300, 11 Nov 1940
Main direction of Swordfish
torpedo attacks

Mar Piccolo

Cruiser   Cruiser

Second wave

Torpedo nets

TARANTO

Mar Grande

Fiume

Zara

Quilio

Littorio

Cesare

First waves

Gorizia

San Pietro

Balloon barrage

Vittorio Veneto

Doria

Cavour

San Paulo

Diga di Tarantola

Oil storage depot

Diga di San Vito

SHIPS CRIPPLED

0   1 MILE

The Royal Navy faced a difficult task in the Mediterranean, where the well-equipped and modern Italian Navy enjoyed a position from which it could strike at will. British forces were split between Gibraltar (Force H) and Alexandria, with Malta at the center – a key position, but highly vulnerable. Only light and submarine naval forces were based on Malta, and Mediterranean Fleet commander Sir Andrew Cunningham was constantly seeking ways to enhance the British position in the Mediterranean through flexible use of his surface ships, including a limited number of carriers.

Cunningham's forces scored several successes against the Italian Navy in chance encounters during July 1940, and plans were laid to attack the Italian fleet in harbor at Taranto. On the night of 11 November, 21 Swordfish torpedo-bombers were launched from the carrier *Illustrious*: all but two returned, having sunk the new battleship *Littorio* and two modernized battleships and inflicted heavy damage on other craft. It was a major coup for the British, and soon followed by another successful strike at Cape Matapan, Greece.

Italian naval forces moved toward Greece in late March 1941, to interdict convoys carrying British troops to assist the Greeks during the Axis invasion of the Balkans, then imminent. On 27 March, RAF scouts reported three Italian cruisers heading east, and Admiral Cunningham put to sea from Alexandria. Three battleships, an aircraft carrier and destroyer escorts comprised his force, which was to rendezvous south of Crete with Vice-Admiral H D Pridham-Wippell commanding a force of four cruisers and four destroyers.

The principal target among the Italian force converging south of Crete was the battleship *Vittorio Veneto*, the pride of Mussolini's fleet. Air strikes were launched against her, but only one torpedo found its mark. Then the Italian cruiser *Pola* was heavily damaged, and the heavy cruisers *Zara* and *Fiume* were sent back to help; all three were destroyed.

The remainder of the Italian force fled back to its bases, including the *Vittorio Veneto*, which found safe harbor at Taranto to the disappointment of Admiral Cunningham and his men.

Above: The successful night attack on the Italian fleet in Taranto on 11 November 1940 mounted by 21 Swordfish torpedo-bombers from HMS Illustrious.
Below: A second blow was dealt to Italian naval might at Cape Matapan on 28 March 1941.
Following pages: HMS Barham, *a battleship of the Allied Mediterranean fleet, at Gibraltar.*

AIR STRIKES BY BLENHEIMS FROM MALEME AND TORPEDO BOMBERS FROM FORMIDABLE

TIMES SHOWN ARE THOSE ON 28 MARCH 1941

0   NAUTICAL MILES   50

GREECE

C. Matapan

Crete

Maleme Airfield

Garibaldi and Abruzzi to Brindisi   2359

Light forces (Pridham-Wippell) cruisers: Orion, Ajax, Gloucester, Perth and 4 destroyers

GÁVDHOS

cruisers: Trieste, Trento, Bolzano and 3 destroyers

Vittorio Veneto to Taranto   1700   2359

Vittorio Veneto

cruisers: Zara, Pola, Fiume, Garibaldi, Abruzzi and 4 destroyers

2300   1515   2100   0600   0700   0722   0722

1830   1200   1100   0812 opens fire

1510 1450 1420   1200   1200

1700   1205   0855 cease fire

1520   1200

Battle Squadron (Cunningham) Warspite, Barham, Valiant, carrier Formidable and 9 destroyers

2100 Zara, Fiume and 4 destroyers turn back to assist Pola

2230 Battlegroup sinks Zara, Fiume, Pola and 2 destroyers

1930 Torpedo bombers from Formidable score hit on Pola

1058-1127 Light forces in action with Vittorio Veneto

0812-0855 Light forces in action with Trieste division

MEDITERRANEAN SEA

The Malta Convoys

The British island fortress of Malta was in serious straits by mid 1942. Its location astride Axis supply lines made it the target of incessant air attack, and its own supply lines were increasingly tenuous. Convoys to Malta had to be suspended in July due to their heavy losses. It was clear that Malta could not hold out against both the Luftwaffe and the Italian Regia Aeronautica without food or fuel, and Operation Pedestal was mounted as a desperate effort to convoy supplies from England.

Twenty warships under command of Vice-Admiral E N Syfret left the Clyde on 3 August with 14 merchantmen, 32 destroyers and various smaller craft. The aircraft carrier *Furious* accompanied the group with a cargo of fighter planes for Malta's RAF squadron. On 10 September, when the convoy passed through the Strait of Gibraltar in fog, a dummy convoy was dispatched from Port Said toward Malta as a diversion. Next day it returned to port, having failed to distract Axis leaders from the main operation, which was shadowed by reconnaissance aircraft from the morning of 11 September. That afternoon *Furious* flew her planes off to Malta and turned back, and the Axis made its first overt move in the form of a U-boat attack on the carrier *Eagle*, which was sunk.

The next day brought heavy Allied losses to Axis planes and submarines. The freighter *Deucalion* went down, the destroyer *Foresight* was so badly damaged that she had to be sunk and the *Indomitable*'s flight deck was bombed out of operation. At this point Syfret turned back according to plan, leaving Rear Admiral H M Burrough to escort the convoy the rest of the way with four cruisers and four destroyers. Two of the cruisers were disabled in the next few hours, *Cairo* so badly that she had to be sunk. At dusk, two of the merchantmen were destroyed and one damaged. The American tanker *Ohio* was hit but stayed with the convoy, as did the damaged cruiser *Kenya*.

Early on the morning of 13 September, five more merchantmen and the cruiser *Manchester* were lost to torpedoes, and renewed air attacks sank *Wairanama* and did additional damage to *Ohio*, with its irreplaceable fuel cargo. By the time light forces from Malta met the convoy, all but five of the merchantmen had been sunk, along with one aircraft carrier, two cruisers and a destroyer. But the fuel and other supplies that got through enabled Malta to hold on.

Above: The hazardous passage to Malta. Below: The damaged tanker HMS Ohio *limps toward port with destroyer escort. Right: General Eisenhower (left) on Malta with Viscount Gort, the island's governor.*

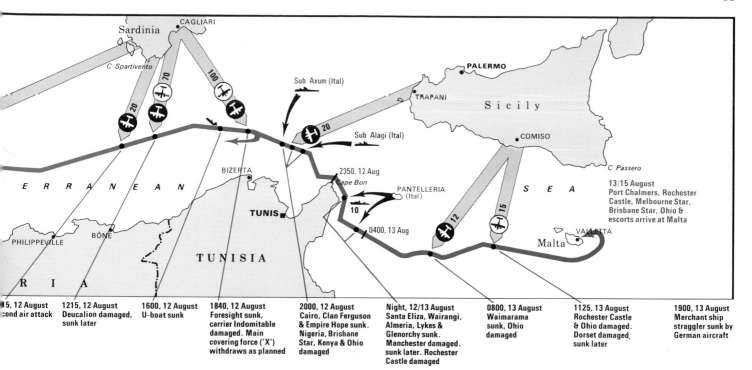

| 5, 12 August cond air attack | 1215, 12 August Deucalion damaged, sunk later | 1600, 12 August U-boat sunk | 1840, 12 August Foresight sunk, carrier Indomitable damaged. Main covering force ('X') withdraws as planned | 2000, 12 August Cairo, Clan Ferguson & Empire Hope sunk. Nigeria, Brisbane Star, Kenya & Ohio damaged | Night, 12/13 August Santa Eliza, Wairangi, Almeria, Lykes & Glenorchy sunk. Manchester damaged. sunk later. Rochester Castle damaged | 0800, 13 August Waimarama sunk, Ohio damaged | 1125, 13 August Rochester Castle & Ohio damaged. Dorset damaged, sunk later | 1900, 13 August Merchant ship straggler sunk by German aircraft |

El Alamein: The First Battle

Below: The German tanks advance, with Italian support.
Right: The first Battle of El Alamein.
Below right: General Grant tanks of the Allied 22nd Armored Brigade advance south of El Alamein.

After the fall of Tobruk, Rommel was promoted to Field Marshal, a status that strengthened his argument for advancing to Egypt at once. (The original Axis plan called for a halt while naval and air forces massed to invade Malta.) Using the supplies newly captured at Tobruk, Rommel crossed the Egyptian frontier and attacked the British at Mersa Matruh (26-27 June), where Eighth Army was now under tactical command of General Claude Auchinleck, Commander in Chief, Middle East. The British could not contain the German advance and retreated to the next defensible position – a line south from the small rail station of El Alamein.

Auchinleck had few reserve units with which to prepare his position from El Alamein, near the coast, to the Qattara Depression, an area of wilderness that was considered almost impassable. His depleted forces took their positions along this line to bar the way to the Nile. Meanwhile, Rommel's forces had also been much reduced in recent battles – to some 2000 German infantry and 65 tanks – while fuel and other supplies were dwindling (these had consisted largely of booty captured at Tobruk and Mersa Matruh).

Eighth Army's artillery units were instrumental in repelling the first German and Italian attacks on 2-4 July; their coordination was much better than it had been under General N M Ritchie from whom Auchinleck had assumed command. The British Commander in Chief was now in a position to essay some limited counterattacks, whose targets were Italian rather than German divisions. This choice was deliberate, as it compelled Rommel to waste fuel in widespread efforts to assist his Italian cohorts.

The *Sabratha* unit fell to the 9 Australian Division on 10-11 July, and the British recovered Tell el Eisa as a result.

Larger Allied efforts were mounted in the Ruweisat Ridge area, where opposing forces grappled to an exhausted standstill. Both sides were simply worn out, and Auchinleck's refusal to continue the attacks known collectively as the First Battle of El Alamein was to cost him his command.

Below: The Allied retreat along the Mediterranean coast to El Alamein.

EIGHT ARMY
◼ CORPS HEADQUARTERS
◼ DIVISIONAL HEADQUARTERS
▸ BRIGADE HEADQUARTERS
(POSITIONS ARE THOSE ON MORNING OF 1 JULY)

0 MILES 10
0 KILOMETERS 16

Tell el Eisa
Italian XXI Corps

10/11 July,
Auchinleck's newly arrived
9 Australian Div recovers
Tell el Eisa

DAK
Tell el Makh Khad
90 Lt Div
EL ALAMEIN
3 S Afr Bde
El Alamein perimeter

TELL EL AQQAQIR
Italian XX Corps
Italian X Corps

15 Pz Div
21 Pz Div
Miteirya Ridge

1 July,
4 Armd Bde arrives
just ahead of 90 Lt Div

4 Armd Bde
1 S Afr Div
ALAM EL ONSOL
2 S Afr Bde Col
XXX Corps

Deir el Abyad
1800 hrs,
1 July
Deir el Shein
18 Ind Bde
Pt.63
Ruweisat Ridge
1 S Afr Bde Col
22 Armd Bde
Pt 64
1 Armd Div

El Mreir
Ariete Div
3 July
2/4 July,
Rommel's attacks
twice repulsed
Deir el Hima
Alam Halfa Ridge

6 NZ Bde
Bab el Qattara
NZ Artillery
Alam Nayil
NZ Infantry

XIII Corps
Deir el Munassib
NZ Div

7 Motor Bde

9 Ind Bde
5 Ind Div
Naqb Abu Dweis
El Taqa Plateau
7 Armd Div
Barrel Track
Qaret el Himeimat

Qattara Depression

To Alexandria, 55 miles
To Cairo, 130 miles

The Battle of Alam Halfa

In August 1942 Churchill arrived in the Middle East to make changes. General Harold Alexander replaced Auchinleck as Commander in Chief, and General Bernard Montgomery took charge of Eighth Army. Less than three weeks later, he would face Rommel's last attempt to break through the position at El Alamein.

Montgomery's defensive plan was based loosely upon Auchinleck's: to hold the Alam Halfa Ridge and counter a German threat in the South with 7 Armored Division. Rommel used the tactic this plan had anticipated when, on 30 August, his main attacks swung south of the British positions with the object of turning north again beyond Alam Halfa to surround Eighth Army. The presence of 7 Armored Division on the right flank

forced him to turn north earlier than he had intended, with the result that DAK failed to break through the Alam Halfa position. Harassing air attacks and a shortage of fuel compounded Rommel's difficulties. His 15 Panzer Division tried to outflank 22 Armored Brigade on 1 September, but this effort was stymied by an improved British antitank system. Axis forces pulled back to prepare a deep

Below: A Vickers gun noses over the barricades.
Right: The Axis attack on Alam Halfa failed to achieve its objectives.
Below right: Rommel's staff confer as the Allied defense turns into counterattack.

defensive position between the Qattara Depression and the sea.

Rommel had to hold the new line of defense or be overwhelmed – he lacked both the vehicles and the fuel for a mobile battle. By the same token he could not retreat. On 6 September, Axis forces were back where they had started, committed to an immediate counterattack for every foot of disputed ground.

El Alamein: The Second Battle

In his new command, General Montgomery lived up to his reputation as a careful planner who emphasized both training and morale. Eighth Army had suffered many changes of fortune and command in the North African Theater, and morale had eroded to a serious degree. Failures of co-operation and confidence had resulted in faulty operations, and Montgomery addressed himself to rebuilding Eighth Army into an optimum fighting unit. At the same time, he was amassing a force superior to the Germans' in every respect: troops, tanks, guns and aircraft.

The Germans were well dug in along a line between the sea and the Qattara Depression, and Montgomery's plan was to attack north of the Miteirya Ridge. The infantry of XXX Corps was to push forward to the Oxalic Line and open corridors through the minefields for passage of the X Corps' Sherman tanks, which were finally proving a match for the German Mark IV. Axis forward defenses were manned largely by Italian troops, and Rommel was hospitalized in Germany; he did not arrive until 25 October, when the battle was underway. General Stumme commanded in his absence.

The British infantry made a good start toward its objectives on 24 October, but it proved impossible to move the tanks forward as planned. The German 21st Panzer Division was kept out of the main battle for several days by diversionary efforts from XIII Corps, and the German defense suffered as a result of General Stumme's death from a heart attack during the first day of fighting. The Axis fuel shortage had become critical with the sinking of two tankers in Tobruk Harbor.

When Rommel returned to North Africa, he launched a series of unsuccessful counterattacks that ended on 3 November, when the British armor began to break through into open ground. Hitler at first forbade a withdrawal, but by 4 November Axis losses had made it inevitable. Rommel and his remaining forces made good their retreat.

Above right: The attack plan for corridors to be driven through Axis minefields to provide safe passage for Allied tanks.
Right: General Montgomery directs operations at El Alamein. On his right is General Sir Brian Horrocks.

SIDI ABD EL RAHMAN
90 Lt Div
164 Div
Littorio
Division and
Tell el Eisa
Tell el Aqqaqir
9 Aust Div
XXX
1 Armd Div corridor
X Corps
Rahman Track
Kidney Ridge
51 (H) Div
Corps
N.Z. Div
15 Panzer
10 Armd Div corridor
S. Afr Div
Miteirya Ridge

AXIS MINEFIELDS
'OPERATION LIGHTFOOT'
'OXALIC'; XXX CORPS' FINAL OBJECTIVE (0310 HRS, 24 OCT)
'PIERSON'; X CORPS' FIRST OBJECTIVE (DAWN, 24 OCT)
'SKINFLINT'; X CORPS' FINAL OBJECTIVE

| 0 | MILES | 10 |
| 0 | KILOMETERS | 16 |

Above: Italian infantrymen in the field at El Alamein.
Right: The second battle saw the Eighth Army repel Axis attacks.

AXIS ARMOR
AXIS INFANTRY
AXIS MINEFIELDS
MAIN AXIS MOVEMENTS
WESTERN EDGE OF EIGHTH ARMY'S MINEFIELDS
EIGHTH ARMY ATTACKS

0   MILES   20
0   KILOMETERS   30

EL DABA

Trieste Div

GHAZAL   90 Lt Div
28 Oct

SIDI ABD EL RAHMAN

29 Oct

2130 hrs, 23 October,
Eighth Army launches attack

28/29 Oct

15 Pz Div

164 Div

Tell el Eisa

Tell el Aqqaqir   1/2 Nov

Kidney Ridge   9 Aust Div

51 (H) Div

4 November,
X Corps' breakthrough

NZ Div

Rahman Track

Littorio Div

Miteiriya Ridge

EL ALAMEIN

XXX Corps
(Leese)

X Corps
(Lumsden)

Trento Div

1 S Afr Div

24 Oct

1 Armd Div

10 Armd Div

Bologna Div

4 Ind Div

Ruweisat Ridge

Ramke Para Bde

Brescia Div

50 Div

21 Pz Div and Ariete Div

XIII Corps
(Horrocks)

25 Oct   44 Div

7 Armd Div

Folgore Div

25 Oct

Naqb Abu Dweis

El Taqa Plateau   Pavia Div

Qaret el Himeimat   1 Free French Bde

Qattara Depression

Operation Torch

On 8 November 1942, four days after Rommel began to retreat from El Alamein, American and British forces made a series of landings in French North Africa. This operation, code-named Torch, was the first real Allied effort of the war. It was hoped that the numerous Vichy French forces in North Africa would not resist the landings, and the US had undertaken diplomatic missions to local French leaders with this object in view. (Anglo-French relations were still embittered by the events of 1940.) Despite these efforts, sporadic French opposition delayed planned Allied attacks on Casablanca and Mehdia, and two destroyers were lost off Algiers. However, the weakest point of the Allied plan was its failure to occupy Tunisia in the first landings. German troops began to arrive there on 9 November to cover Rommel's retreat and formed a defensive perimeter.

The Allied capture of Vichy leader Admiral Darlan at Algiers helped diminish resistance from French forces; fewer than 2000 casualties were incurred in the three main landing areas. The largest difficulty was pushing the considerable Allied force the 400 miles to Tunis before the Germans could pour in troops and aircraft from Sicily. This they did with great speed, on instructions from Hitler and Commander in Chief Mediterranean

Field Marshal Kesselring. Allied forces under General Dwight D Eisenhower, American Commander in Chief of the Torch operation, were stopped short in Tunisia by early December.

Below: US troops march on Algiers' Maison Blanche airfield.
Bottom: The Operation Torch landings.
Right: The Allied push into Tunisia.
Below right: The Germans reinforce.

ALLIES
ALLIED AIRBORNE LANDINGS
GERMAN
BRITISH V CORPS FRONT, 1 JANUARY 1943

MILES 20
KILOMETRES 30

HEIGHT IN FEET
OVER 7000
5000-7000
1000-5000
UNDER 1000

C Serrat

BIZERTA
Sidi Ahmed
Lake of Bizerta
Garaet Achkel
Tindja

9 November, German advance parties land

Gulf of Tunis

26 Nov, 36 Bde TAMERA
30 Nov, 36 Bde repulsed
Dj Azzag
SEDJENANE
Dj Ajred
MATEUR

18 Nov, German attack repulsed
DJEBEL ABIOD

10 November, Germans establish bridgehead

26 Nov, Allies attack airfield

El Aouina

16 Nov, Hart Force
17 Nov, 36 Bde

18 Nov, 1 Para Bn
SIDI NSIR
17 Nov

27 Nov, 1 Para Bn

DJEDEIDA
TEBOURBA
27/29 Nov, 5 Northampton Regt
1 E Surrey Regt

TUNIS

TÁBARKA

Hart Force
36 Bde

T   U   N   I   S   I   A

26/27 Nov, Bn,11 Bde

Longstop
Medjerda

ST CYPRIEN

First Army
(Anderson)

BÉJA

25 Nov, 11 Bde

MEDJEZ EL BAB

25 Nov

1 Dec, 2 Para Bn retires

Oudna
1 Dec

30 Nov

SOUK EL KHEMIS

SLOUGHIA

29 Nov, German road block

SOUK EL ARBA
16 Nov, 1 Para Bn
18 Nov, Blade Force

TEBOURSOUK   23 Nov
Blade Force
→ To Le Kef 40 miles

29 Nov, 2 Para Bn
Depienne

BOU ARADA

PONT DU FAHS

56 Recce Regt

From Tripoli to Tunis

Eighth Army's pursuit of Rommel's forces was hampered by weather and supply problems. It took Montgomery almost three weeks to reach Agedabia (23 November 1942), and he had to halt there until he was resupplied. Soon after, the short-lived German position at El Agheila was outflanked and the race toward Tunisia resumed.

The port of Tripoli offered the British hope of alleviating their supply problems, but the Germans got there first and did as much damage as they could to port installations before pushing on to Tunisia. The British reached Tripoli on 23 January 1943, and it was not until mid-March that the port began to function effectively as a pipeline for British supplies. Meanwhile, Axis forces had consolidated behind the Mareth Line after inflicting 10,000 casualties on Allied troops from the Torch landings at the Battle of Kasserine. Rommel now faced Montgomery's Eighth Army in his last battle in Africa – a bitter fight that raged from 6 to 27 March. Axis forces were outflanked, and by mid-April had retreated up the coast to form a tight perimeter on the hills around Bizerta and Tunis.

Rommel urged evacuation of German and Italian forces from Africa when he returned to Germany, but his counsel was ignored. Thirteen understrength

Axis divisions sought to defend Tunisia against 19 Allied divisions that had recovered from their earlier reverses to take on an overwhelming superiority in air power and armor. The Allies had 1200 tanks to the Axis' 130, 1500 guns to the Axis' 500.

Hill 609 was hotly contested by American forces seeking access to the so-called Mousetrap Valley leading to the coastal plain. British troops made some progress at Longstop Hill and Peter's Corner, which commanded the Medjerda Valley. Then General Alexander switched experienced units from Eighth Army to V Corps, which made possible a decisive

victory. Allied troops broke through in early May. Tunis fell on the 7th, and five days later Italy's Marshal Messe and Germany's General von Arnim surrendered with some quarter of a million troops. These forces would be sorely missed by Hitler when the Allies launched their invasion of Italy.

Above: The Eighth Army's attempt to progress up Tunisia's east coast was delayed at Wadi Akarit.
Right: The Allied conquest of Tunisia. Bizerta and Tunis fell on 7 May.
Below: The Eighth Army's progress in the wake of El Alamein.

US 9 Div

BIZERTA
7 May

9 May

Lake of
Bizerta FERRYVILLE
7 May

C Serrat

US 9 Div

9 May

Sedjenane

Garaet
Achkel

DJEFNA

MATEUR
3 May

Gulf of Tunis

Cape Bon

US 1 Armd Div

US 1 Div

PROTVILLE
8 May

Medjerda

7 Armd Div

8 May

Cape Bon Peninsula

4 Div

MENZEL
TEMIME
11 May

US II Corps
(Bradley)

Hill 609
1 May ▲

SIDI NSIR

US 34 Div

CHOUIGUI
8 May

DJEDEIDA
8 May

TUNIS
7 May

US 34 Div

TEBOURBA

US 1 Div

6 Armd Div

HAMMAM LIF
8 May

MENZEL
BOU ZELFA

Longstop
26 Apr

▲ Dj Bou Aoukaz
5 May

MASSICAULT
6 May

7 May LA MOHAMMEDIA

4 Div

KORBA

BÉJA

HEIDOUS
78 Div

Gueriat
el Atach

1 Div
4 Ind Div
4 Div

Peter's Corner

1 Armd Div

6 Armd Div

MEDJEZ EL BAB
7 Armd Div
6 Armd Div

• KSAR TYR

Brit V Corps
(Allfrey)

20/21 Apr.

24 Apr

30 Apr

9 May

ST MARIE DU ZIT
11 May

10 May
• HAMMAMET

GOUBELLAT

Brit IX Corps
(Crocker/Horrocks)

1 Armd Div

23 Apr

Sebkret el Kourzia

46 Div

25 Apr

PONT DU FAHS
7 May

▲ Dj Zaghouan

18 April,
1 Armd Div
End April,
7 Armd Div
4 Ind Div
to First Army
from Eighth Army

TEBOURSOUK

BOU ARADA

xxxx

Dj Garci

50 Div

First Army
(Anderson)

xxx

Brit IX Corps

xxx

18 Army Group
(Alexander)

Div d'Oran

Div du
Maroc

xxxx

TAKROUNA

51 (H) Div

NZ Div • ENFIDAVILLE

Fr XIX Corps
(Koeltz)

First Army
Eighth Army

Eighth Army
(Montgomery)

FRONT LINE, 22 APRIL 1943
ALLIED ATTACKS 22/30 APRIL
" " 1/7 MAY
" " 8/11 MAY
GERMAN COUNTERATTACKS

HEIGHT IN FEET

OVER 1800
1200-1800
600-1200
UNDER 600

0 — MILES — 25
0 — KILOMETRES — 40

---

400   300   200   100   MILES   0

ROMMEL'S DEFENSE POSITIONS
EIGHTH ARMY'S ADVANCE

M E D I T E R R A N E A N   S E A

CYRENE

DERNA

a Balbia

khdar

GAZALA

TOBRUK 13 Nov

MECHILI

BARDIA

SIDI BARRANI 9 Nov

Halfaya Pass
11 Nov

MERSA MATRÛH 7 Nov

ALEXANDRIA

PORT SAID

Brit X and XXX Corps

FUKA

SIDI ABD
EL RAHMAN

Suez
Canal

C y r e n a i c a

4 Nov 1942
Rommel begins
to retreat

EL ALAMEIN

CAIRO

SUEZ

Qattara Depression

Nile

E G Y P T

600   500   400   300   200   100   KILOMETERS   0

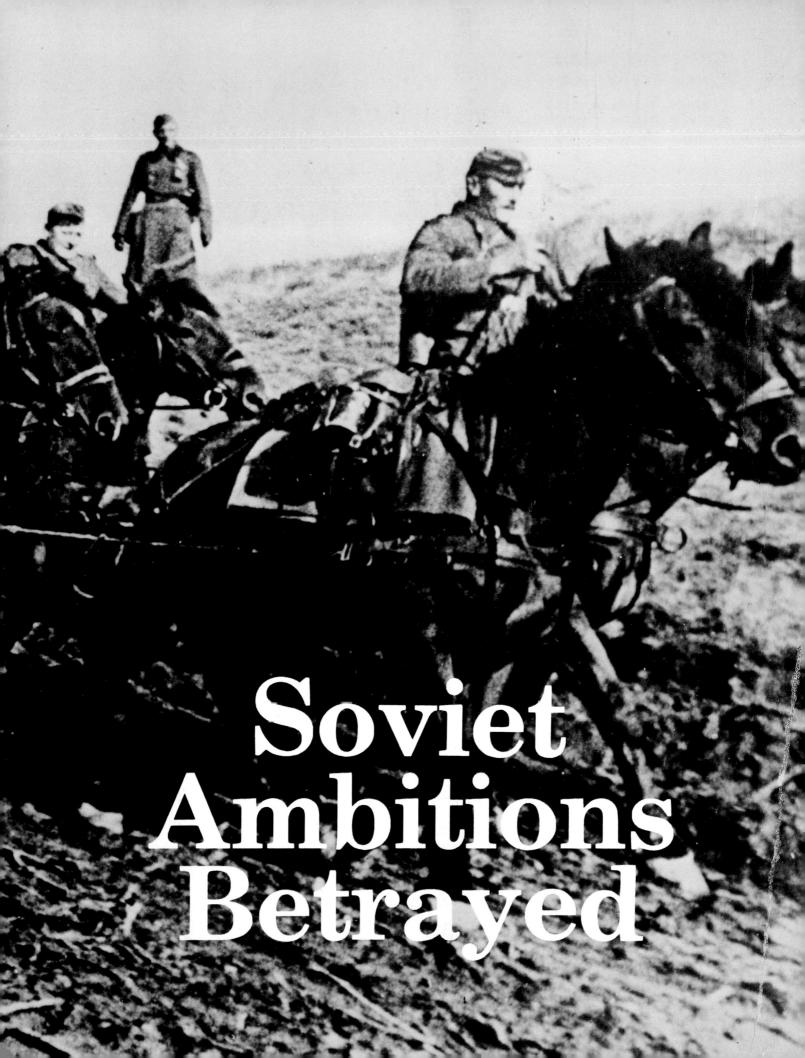

Soviet Ambitions Betrayed

The Winter War: Finland, 1939-40

On 30 November 1939, the Soviet Union invaded Finland, after failing to obtain territorial concessions demanded in early October. Five different Soviet armies crossed the Russo-Finnish frontier on four major fronts, but the conquest of this small neighboring nation proved much more difficult than had been foreseen. Deep snow and heavy forest forced Russian tanks and transports to stay on the roads, where they were easy targets for the mobile, well-trained Finnish ski troops. Russian convoys were shot up and separated, and formations were isolated and defeated in detail. The Finns never had more than nine divisions in the field, with few guns and almost no tanks. But their confidence was high, and they had the advantage of fighting on familiar ground with tactics suited to the terrain.

By 31 January 1940, the Russians had made deep penetrations in the north by dint of superior numbers, but the Mannerheim Line, on the Karelian Isthmus, was holding on. The Seventh and Thirteenth Soviet Armies assaulted this line from 1 through 13 February with forces that included six tank brigades and 21 infantry divisions. A massive bombardment preceded these attacks, which achieved a breakthrough in mid-February. The Finns were forced to surrender, and to cede the Karelian Isthmus and considerable territory in the north. They would seek to make good these losses the following year in an alliance with Nazi Germany.

The Finnish fight was solitary and ultimately hopeless, because the British and French Governments feared to arouse Soviet hostility by involving themselves. Nevertheless, the Russo-Finnish War had far-reaching consequences in the international community. As a result of it, the French Government fell due to dissension about helping the Finns, and the League of Nations was thoroughly discredited. Hitler formed a false impression of Soviet inefficiency that probably influenced his decision to turn on his Russian ally. And the Red Army was awakened to deep-seated internal problems that became subject to reform in the months that followed.

Previous pages: The Wehrmacht advance with difficulty along a muddy Russian road, 1941.
Below: The Russians breach Finland's Mannerheim Line in February.
Right: Soviet soldiers dismantle Finnish anti-tank obstacles.

RUSSIAN ATTACKS: 30 NOV, 1939/31 JAN, 1940
FINNISH COUNTERATTACKS 27 DEC/5 JAN
IV FINNISH ARMY CORPS
CEDED TO RUSSIA AT DATES SHOWN

0   MILES   150
0   KILOMETERS   200

Above: Earlier Soviet penetration in the north and east from November 1939 had met effective Finnish resistance.

Military Balance on the Eastern Front

The German High Command spent almost a year planning the invasion of Russia, code-named Operation Barbarossa. Three different plans were devised, of which the one giving priority to the capture of Leningrad was chosen. German leaders estimated Red Army strength along the frontier at some 155 divisions (in fact, there were 170 within operational distance.) The front was divided in half by the Pripet Marshes. In the north, von Leeb's Army Group North was to aim itself against Leningrad, where it faced an almost equal number of Russian divisions. However, these were deployed so far forward that they were vulnerable to being pushed back against the coast. Von Bock's Army Group Centre, with two Panzer armies, was the strongest German force in the field; facing it was the comparatively weak Red Army West Front. Most Soviet troops were south of the Pripet Marshes, positioned to defend the agricultural and industrial wealth of the Ukraine. Von Rundstedt's Army Group South was to thrust southeast against these forces.

The German plan called for swift penetration deep into Russia in June, to destroy the Red Army long before winter. A massive German buildup began, but Stalin and his advisors were so determined not to give Hitler any excuse to

attack that they ignored all the warning signs. In fact, the Red Army was still on a peacetime footing when the invasion began on 22 June. Most units were widely scattered for summer training; others were too close to the western frontier. The reforms that followed upon the Russo-

Finnish War were far from complete, and there was almost no Russian reserve to deal with deep incursions. The Germans had good reason to be optimistic about the invasion of Russia.

Below: Soviet cavalrymen on the march, 1941. Horse-mounted troops were more mobile than tanks in the severe Russian winter conditions, and were thus more effective than appearances suggested.

Above left: The initial German thrusts to Moscow and Kiev.
Far left: A northern attack was later added to the original two-pronged assault plan.
Left: Hitler finally identified Leningrad as the prime target, and it was this plan of attack that was selected.
Right: The Eastern Front from the Baltic to the Black Sea, showing the relative strengths and dispositions of the two protagonists.

BALTIC SEA

North Front
(Popov)

Latvia

RIGA

EAST PRUSSIA

MEMEL

Eighth Army
(Sobennikov)

Army Group North
(Leeb)
26 divisions
(inc 3 panzer divs)
Luftflotte I

reserve

+ added later for security operations

Eighteenth Army (Küchler)

DANZIG

Lithuania

North-West Front
(F.I. Kuznetsov, then Sobennikov)
24 divisions
(inc 4 tank divs)

KONIGSBERG

Fourth Panzergruppe
(Hoeppner)

Eleventh Army
(Morosov)

Sixteenth Army
(Busch)

KAUNAS

Vistula

Third Panzergruppe
(Hoth)

SUWALKI

Third Army
(V.I. Kuznetsov)

Ninth Army
(Strauss)

West Front
(Pavlov, then Timoshenko)
38 divisions
(inc 8 tank divs)

Army Group Centre
(Bock)
51 divisions
(inc 9 panzer divs)
Luftflotte II

reserve

WARSAW

Fourth Army
(Kluge)

BIALYSTOK

Bug

Tenth Army
(Golubev)

MINSK

Thirteenth Army
(Filatov)
Front reserve at Minsk

POLAND

Fourth Army
(Korobkov)

BREST LITOVSK

Belorussia

Second Panzergruppe
(Guderian)

LUBLIN

PINSK

Pripet Marshes

Sixth Army (Reichenau)

KRAKOW

Pripet

First Panzergruppe
(Kleist)

Fifth Army
(Potapov)

Seventeenth Army
(Stülpnagel)

ROVNO

Slovakia

PRZEMYSL

LVOV

Sixth Army
(Muzychenko)

Pre-war Polish boundary

South-West Front
(Kirponos, then Budenny)
56 divisions
(inc 16 tank divs)

reserve

Carpathian Mts.

Twenty-sixth Army
(Kostenko)

HUNGARY

Hungarian divs

Twelfth Army
(Ponedelin)

CHERNOVTSY

Ukraine

Army Group South
(Rundstedt)
59 divisions
(inc 5 panzer divs,
14 Rumanian divs &
2 Hungarian divs)
Luftflotte IV

reserve

Rum Third Army
(Dumitrescu)

Eighteenth Army
(Smirnov)

Eleventh Army
(Schobert)

JASSY

Prut

Moldavia

South Front
(Tyulenev)
16 divisions
(inc 4 tank divs)

Rum Fourth Army
(Ciuperca)

Ninth Army
(Cherevichenko)

ODESSA

RUMANIA

GALATI

Danube

ARMOURED DIVISIONS

OTHER DIVISIONS, including motorised infantry (in Panzergruppen) and cavalry

0 MILES 150

0 KILOMETRES 200

BLACK SEA

Operation Barbarossa: 1941

German forces achieved almost total surprise in their 22 June invasion of Soviet territory, which was preceded by a devastating air attack that all but wiped out the Red Air Force. Fourth Panzer Group took a series of northern objectives that brought it to the Luga by 14 July. Army Group Centre sealed off Russian forces at Bialystok and Gorodische, taking 300,000 prisoners and 2500 tanks in a week's operations. Army Group South faced the greatest resistance in the Ukraine, where the Russian Fifth Army counterattacked on 10 July to prevent an assault on Kiev.

This development incited Hitler to divert Army Group Centre from its attack on Moscow via Smolensk into the Ukraine offensive. Second Army and Heinz Guderian's Second Panzer Group were ordered south to destroy the Soviet Fifth Army and surround Kiev. Guderian was radically opposed to abandoning the Moscow offensive, but he turned south on 23 August as ordered. An unsuccessful Russian counteroffensive failed to halt the German advance north of Gomel, and the Soviet South-West Front suffered heavy losses every time it gave battle. Many divisions were trapped in pockets and destroyed piecemeal, while at Kiev alone, half a million Red soldiers were captured.

By mid November the Germans had seized Rostov and the Perekop Isthmus, which commanded the Crimea. In the center, their victories at Smolensk and Bryansk had enabled them to capture Orel, Tula and Vyazma. The Baltic States had been occupied, and the Finnish alliance had helped open the way to Leningrad.

FINLAND

SWEDEN

HELSINKI

3 Dec 1941
Evacuated by Russia

HANKO (USSR)

Gulf of Finland

TURKU

VIPURI

LAKE
LADOGA

Twenty-third
Army

Forty-second &
Fifty-second Armies

VOLKHOV

Eighth Army

TIKHVIN

Fifty-fourth Army

Fourth Army

Fifty-ninth Army

Second Shock Army

NOVGOROD

Eleventh Army

North-West Front
(Voroshilov)

Thirty-
fourth Army

Third Shock Army

Twenty-seventh Army

KALININ

Twenty-second Army

Twenty-ninth
Army

MOSCOW

BALTIC
SEA

TALLINN

NARVA

Estonia

TARTU

L Peipus

PSKOV

OSTROV

STARAYA
RUSS

L Ilmen

KHOLM

OSTASHKOV

VENTSPILS

Latvia

RIGA

REZEKNE

Dvina

IDRITSA

VELIKIYE
LUKI

BELYY

RZHEV

Army Group
North (Leeb)

MEMEL

Eighteenth
Army

Eighth
Army

Lithuania

DAUGAVPILS

POLOTSK

VELIZH

Thirtieth Army

Nineteenth Army

Sixteenth Army

EAST
PRUSSIA

Fourth Pzgrp
Sixteenth Army

Ninth Army
Third Pzgrp

KAUNAS

Eleventh
Army

VILNYUS

VITEBSK

YARTSEVO

SMOLENSK

VYAZMA

Thirty-second Army

Twentieth Army

KALUGA

Novi Borisov

*Moscow
Highway*

ORSHA

MOGILEV

YELNYA

Twenty-fourth Army

TULA

Army Group
Center (Bock)

Third
Army

GRODNO

MINSK

Berezina

ROSLAVL

Twenty-eighth
Army

West Front
(Timoshenko)

BIALYSTOK

Tenth
Army

GORODISHCHE

NOVO
BYKHOV

Forty-third
Army

WARSAW

Fourth
Army

Belorussia

Sozh

KRICHE

Fiftieth Army

BRYANSK

BREST-LITOVSK

PINSK

Pripet

BOBRUYSK

GOMEL

STARODUB

OREL

Fourth Army
Second Pzgrp

Twenty-
first Army

RECHITSA

Second
Pzgrp

Third Army

POLAND

Pripet Marshes

MOZYR

NOVGOROD
SEVERSKI

Thirteenth
Army

KURSK

Bug

Vistula

KOVEL

KOROSTEN

Fifth Army

CHERNIGOV

Desna

KONOTOP

South-West
Front (Budenny)

Sixth Army
First Pzgrp

Fifth Army

ROVNO

BAKHMACH

Second
Army

Fortieth
Army

Seventeenth
Army

LWOW

Sixth Army

TERNOPOL

ZHITOMIR

BERDICHEV

KAZATIN

KIEV

Thirty-
seventh
Army

LOKHVITSA

Twenty-first
Army

KHARKOV

Slovakia

Carpathian

Twenty-sixth
Army

Dniestr

First Pzgrp

CHERKASSY

POLTAVA

Thirty-
eighth
Army

Army Group
South (Rundstedt)

CHERNOVTSY

KAMENETS-PODOLSKY

UMAN

VINNITSA

Ukraine

PERVOMAYSK

KREMENCHUG

Sixth
Army

DNEPROPETROVSK

Twelfth
Army

HUNGARY

Twelfth Army

Rum Third
Army

Eighteenth
Army

Eleventh
Army

Moldavia

KISHINEV

Prut

Seventeenth
Army

KRIVOY ROG

Eleventh
Army

Dniepr

ZAPOROZHYE

Eighteenth
Army

MELITOPOL

Rum Fourth
Army

Ninth
Army

ODESSA
16 Oct

NIKOLAYEV

PEREKOP

Ninth
Army

RUMANIA

BUCHAREST

Fifty-first
Army

*Sea of
Azov*

Crimea

SEVASTOPOL

Danube

CONSTANTA

BLACK SEA

▼▼▼ ▼▼▼▼ STALIN LINE
━━━━━ FRONT LINE, 21 JUNE 1941
‒ ‒ ‒ ‒   „   „   9 JULY
‒·‒·‒·‒   „   „   1 SEPTEMBER
▪▪▪▪▪   „   „   30 SEPTEMBER
←━━ RUSSIAN COUNTERATTACKS
▨▨▨ TRAPPED RUSSIAN POCKETS

0   MILES   200
0   KILOMETERS   300

The Finnish Front

The 1941 alliance with Germany brought significant improvements in Finland's forces. Mobilization and training systems were revamped, as the Finns prepared to regain the territory lost to Russia the previous year by expediting the German assault in the north. Marshal Carl von Mannerheim, hero of the Russo-Finnish War, would lead first the army and then the state for the balance of World War II.

Joint German-Finnish attacks began on 19 June 1941, with early successes around Lake Ladoga. The Russians were outflanked there and began to withdraw by water, until the Finns had pursued to a point near their former frontier (1 September). On the Karelian Isthmus, another attack reached Vuosalmi on 16 August, but was stopped short of Leningrad by a second Russian retreat. At this point Mannerheim called a halt: having regained the territory lost in the previous year, he was reluctant to become more deeply involved in the attack on Russia.

Offensives did not resume until several days later, when attacks north of Lake Ladoga and against the Murmansk railway achieved their objectives. Then the Russian resistance grew increasingly stronger, and by early December the Finns were on the defensive. The front line stabilized along an axis east of the 1939 Russo-Finnish boundary.

The Attack on Leningrad

German Army Group North, commanded by General Wilhelm von Leeb, arrived near Leningrad on 1 September 1941. The Germans had decided not to storm the city, but to isolate it and starve out its defenders. Artillery bombardments began immediately, and within two weeks Leningrad had been cut off entirely from overland communication with the rest of Russia.

The city had only a month's supply of food – heavily rationed – and starvation set in by October. The following month, 11,000 died of hunger. Meager supplies continued to come in by barge across Lake Ladoga in the early fall, but on 9 November the Germans took Tikhvin, the point of origin, and ice on the lake made navigation impossible. Four weeks later, the Russians opened a new 'Life-line' road from Zaborie to Lednevo, but winter weather and difficult terrain slowed supply trucks to a crawl.

Thousands more had succumbed to starvation in Leningrad by early December, when the Red Army's counteroffensive began to make itself felt. Tikhvin was recaptured, and the Germans were pushed back to the Volkhov River. The Russians repaired the railroad and opened an ice road across the lake, which was now frozen solidly enough to bear the weight of trucks. By Christmas Day, it was possible to increase the bread ration in Leningrad. But relief came too late for many: on that same day, almost 4000 died of starvation.

Above: Supply routes to the besieged city of Leningrad.
Below: Finnish members of the Waffen-SS in action.

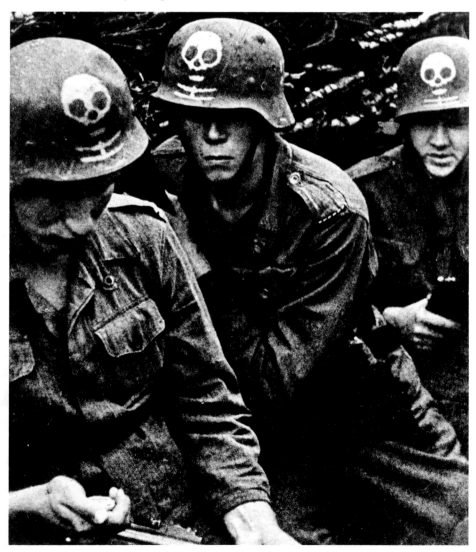

74

Moscow – Strike and Counterstrike

Below: The German Army Group South pushes to capture the Ukraine, but is forced to withdraw to the Mius River.
Bottom: Muscovites dig defense lines around the capital, 1941.
Right: The German assault on Moscow.

After capturing Kiev, the Germans redeployed their forces for the assault on Moscow. They had a superiority of two to one in men and tanks, three to one in the air. Fourteen Panzer divisions were involved in the attacks that converged on Russia's capital beginning 30 September.

By 7 October large pockets of Soviet troops had been cut off around Vyazma and Bryansk. They were systematically destroyed in the next two weeks, after which heavy rains put a serious check on German mobility. The Mozhaisk defense line offered increasing resistance, and by 30 October German forces had bogged down miles from Moscow. Many men and tanks were lost in the frustrating advance through a sea of mud.

When the weather changed, it did little to help the German cause. The freeze that set in hardened the roads, but German soldiers found it difficult to adapt to the extreme cold, which also created new problems with their vehicles. By 27 November, units of the Third Panzer

RUSSIAN

▲▲▲ VYAZMA DEFENSE LINE
△△△ MOZHAISK DEFENSE LINE
▬▬▬ MOSCOW DEFENSE LINES
▨▨▨ TRAPPED POCKETS

0   MILES   100
0   KILOMETERS   160

North-West Front

DEMYANSK

Lake Seliger

Army Group North

Kalinin Front

VISHNI VOLOCHEK

Volga Reservoir

Ninth Army

TOROPETS

OSTASHKOV

Twenty-second Army

SELIZHAROVO

Thirty-first Army

KALININ

DMITROV

ALEKSANDROV

VLADIMIR

Volga

Twenty-ninth Army

OLENINO

STARITSA

RZHEV

NOVO ZAVIDOVSKY

YAKHROMA

KLIN

KRASNAYA POLYANA

Volga Canal

Third Panzergruppe (Hoth)

W. Dvina

BELYY

West Front (Konev)

SYCHEVKA

Reserve Front (Budenny)

VOLOKOLAMSK

SOLNECH-NOGORSK

KHIMKI

Gorky 140 miles

Thirtieth Army

Nineteenth Army

Sixteenth Army

Forty-ninth Army

GZHATSK

BORODINO

ISTRA

Moskva

MOSCOW

Klyazma

DUKHOVSHCHINA

VYAZMA

MOZHAISK

DOROKHOVO

NARO-FOMINSK

PERKHUSHKOVO

PODOLSK

West Front (Konev)

Kazan 370 miles

YARTSEVO

Orsha 10 miles

Moscow Highway

Thirty-second Army

MEDYN

OBNINSKOYE

MALOYAROSLAVETS

KOLOMNA

Dnieper

SMOLENSK

Twentieth Army

YELNYA

YUKHNOV

Ugra

SERPUKHOV

KASHIRA

RYAZAN

Oka

Fourth Army

Twenty-fourth Army

SPAS-DEMENSK

KALUGA

ALEKSIN

VENEV

MIKHAYLOV

Kurbyshev 480 miles

Fourth Panzergruppe (Hoeppner)

ROSLAVL

Warsaw Highway

KIROV

SUKHINICHI

TULA

STALINOGORSK

GORLOVO

Army Group Center (Bock)

Forty-third Army

Upa

TEPLOYE

DANKOV

Second Army

Fiftieth Army

BELEV

BOLKHOV

Oka

MTSENSK

NOVOSIL

YEFREMOV

South-West Front

POCHEP

BRYANSK

Bryansk Front (Yeromenko)

OREL

YELETS

STARODUB

Third Army

LIVNY

Sosna

Thirteenth Army

SEVSK

DMITRIEV-LGOVSKIY

Don

NOVGOROD SEVERSKI

Second Panzer Army ('Panzergruppe Guderian')

GLUKHOV

KURSK

VORONEZH

CHERNIGOV

Desna

Second Panzer Army begins offensive 30 September. All other armies attack 2 October

KONOTOP

Fortieth Army

SUMY

TIM

Army Group South

PRILUKI

OBOYAN

BELGOROD

Kharkov 30 miles

GERMAN

➤ FRONT LINE, 30 SEPTEMBER 1941
➤ OFFENSIVE, 30 SEPT/30 OCT
─·─· FRONT LINE, 10 OCTOBER
─ ─ ─ FRONT LINE, 30 OCT/15 NOV
▷ OFFENSIVE 15 NOV/5 DEC
···· FRONT LINE, 5 DECEMBER
XXXXX ARMY GROUP COMMAND BOUNDARY

Group finally reached the Volga Canal, 19 miles from Moscow center, but they lacked the support for a frontal assault on the city. Elements of the Second Panzer Army had gotten as far as Kashira, but they had to fall back for the same reason.

By 5 December the Germans realized that they could go no farther for the time being. Valuable time has been lost in the capture of Smolensk, whose courageous defenders had helped delay the German advance on Moscow until the dreaded onset of winter. Now the capital could not be completely encircled, and heavy bombing did not offset the failure to close Moscow's window on the east. Fresh Soviet troops began to arrive from Siberia even

as the Germans faced temperatures that plummeted to 40 degrees below zero.

On 8 December Hitler announced a suspension of operations outside Moscow, but the Soviet High Command was not listening. Employing the reserves it had gathered in previous weeks, the Red Army launched a great counteroffensive that recalled the winter of 1812, when Napoleon's forces came to grief on the same ground. Avoiding German strongpoints, the Soviets advanced by infiltration – passing over fields instead of roads, making skillful use of Cossack cavalry, ski troops and guerrilla forces. The Germans were harried from flank and rear, forced from one position after another.

Tanks and planes became inoperable in the extreme cold, and supply lines were tenuous or nonexistent.

With the recapture of Kalinin and Tula, the Russians removed the immediate threat to Moscow. Their offensive drove on into late February, and German troops took refuge in strongly fortified defensive positions (called hedgehogs) in hope of holding out until fresh troops could arrive. Hitler had ordered 'No retreat,' and airborne supplies kept many enclaves going through the winter. But Operation Barbarossa had foundered in the snowfields of Russia. The Soviets were regaining ground from Leningrad to the Crimea.

The Red Army Fights Back

During the fall of 1941, the Russians were able to evacuate much of their factory equipment and many key workers to the east, where they began to rebuild their industrial machine. Railroad equipment was also evacuated, giving the Soviets an edge in the number of locomotives and freight cars per mile of track. The transportation breakdown foreseen by Hitler did not materialize, and Russian troop reserves were built up in Siberia to replace the great losses incurred on the Eastern Front. At the same time, war matériel from the West began to reach Russia via Archangel, Murmansk, Vladivostok and Persia.

Since Operation Barbarossa had been designed to achieve a quick victory during the summer months, German troops had never been equipped for winter warfare. Soviet troops by contrast, were routinely equipped with clothing and vehicles appropriate to the theater of operations. The Soviet Supreme Command (*Stavka*) had rallied from the shock of invasion to make effective use of the huge army that had been so wastefully deployed in June of 1941.

The Russian counteroffensive that began on 5-6 December saw immediate and dramatic gains on many fronts. The siege of Moscow was broken by the Kalinin, West and South-West Fronts (army groups). Supplies began to reach Leningrad in time to avert universal starvation in the besieged city. In the south, the Kerch Isthmus was retaken and the Crimea re-entered with help from the Red Navy. The Russians had gone all the way back to Velikiye Luki and Mozhaisk before they had to rest and regroup in late February 1942.

Opposite: The Red Army launches its counteroffensive.
Right: Russian territory regained by the end of April 1942.
Below: A political meeting of the Russian Twentieth Army near Smolensk.

The Course of Global Conflict: 1939-45

The Treaty of Versailles: Blueprint for Hostilities

Germany had had no part in the negotiations that resulted in the Treaty of Versailles; it was entirely the work of the 32 nations that had been leagued against her in World War I. The 80,000-word draft of the proposed peace treaty was approved by the Allied Peace Congress on 6 May 1919, and German representatives did not even see the document until the following day. They protested bitterly against its terms, and

there were demonstrations all over Germany and a change of government before it was signed.

By the treaty's terms, Germany ceded Alsace-Lorraine to France, the towns of Eupen and Malmédy to Belgium, the city of Memel to Lithuania, and the province of Posen and a 'corridor' through West Prussia to Poland. German Austria, Poland and Czechoslovakia were declared independent. The port city of Danzig was

internationalized as a 'free city,' and the valuable coal region of the Saar passed under League of Nations administration and the economic control of France.

In addition, Germany lost all of its overseas empire, most of its armed forces and control of the Rhineland – which was to be occupied at Germany's expense until the Treaty of Versailles was fully executed. A clause that even some of the victors disputed forced Germany to claim full responsibility for the war and to promise financial reparation 'for all damage done to the civilian population of the Allies and their property.' The initial payment was set at five billion dollars; subsequent reparations were limited only by 'the utmost of [Germany's] ability' to pay. Disarmed, dishonored and heavily mortgaged, the conquered nation embarked upon years of distress and resentment that would culminate in the conflict that was to eclipse even the Great War itself.

Previous page: USS Arizona *explodes at Pearl Harbor, 7 December 1941.*
Opposite: Admiral Chester W Nimitz points the way to Tokyo. Seated (left to right) are General MacArthur, President Roosevelt and Admiral Leahy.
Left: European boundaries before and after Versailles.
Below: The Allied premiers convene in Paris for the Peace Conference in 1919.

German Expansion, 1939-40

The German Army that went to war in 1939 was armed and organized much like that of 1918, but there had been important developments in the interwar years. The Stuka dive bomber now served as a form of mobile artillery at need. Submachine guns offered an advantage in portability over the Vickers and Bren machine guns used by the British. Allied forces had more tanks, but the Germans were much better at using them tactically. German generals knew how to fight the war of movement, while the French were still fixated on their Maginot Line - a static and incomplete system that anticipated a second Verdun. The Germans had no intention of fighting another such action.

The new blitzkrieg style of German warfare rolled over Poland, Norway, Denmark and France in a matter of months. The British Army was shattered by the French campaign, but the evacuation from Dunkirk and the crucial weeks bought by the Battle of Britain staved off invasion of the British Isles. Mussolini took advantage of Allied defeats to enter the war on the German side, but Italian

March 1939 Annexed by Germany

August 1939 Russo-German non-aggression pact signed

March 1936 Rhineland remilitarized

October 1938 Occupied by Germany

March 1935 Saar Basin to Germany (by plebiscite)

March 1938 Annexed by Germany

March 1939 Occupied by Germany

October 1938 To Hungary

March 1939 To Hungary

May 1939 'Pact of Steel' signed by Germany & Italy

April 1939 Occupied by Italy

GERMANY, 1934
BOUNDARY OF GERMANY, 3 SEPT. 1939
* Slovakia, German protectorate

0 MILES 400
0 KILOMETERS 600

ARCTIC OCEAN

Barents Sea

REYKJAVIK ICELAND

PETSAMO
MURMANSK

NARVIK

White Sea

ARCHANGEL

AXIS PARTNERS : 1939
GERMANY   ITALY
GERMAN SATELLITE
GERMAN OCCUPIED, 27 SEPT 1939
GERMAN OCCUPIED, 23 JUNE 1940
GERMAN FRONT LINES AT DATES SHOWN

SUOMUSSALMI

Ceded to Russia, 1940

FINLAND

30 Nov 1939 -1 March 1940 Russo-Finnish War

MILES   0   500
KILOMETERS   0   800

TRONDHEIM

L. Ladoga

HELSINKI

VIIPURI

LENINGRAD

MOSCOW

BERGEN

3 Sept 1939 Britain & France declare war on Germany

OSLO

STOCKHOLM

TALLINN
ESTONIA

RIGA

R U S S I A

ATLANTIC OCEAN

9 April 1940 Germany invades Norway & Denmark

Baltic Sea

SMOLENSK

VORONEZH

EDINBURGH

NORTH SEA

DENMARK COPENHAGEN

1 Sept 1939 Germany invades Poland

LATVIA

LITHUANIA

June 1940 Annexed by Russia

EIRE DUBLIN

GREAT BRITAIN

LIVERPOOL

DANZIG
KÖNIGSBERG

KAUNAS

MINSK

STALINGRAD

NETH.
AMSTERDAM

HAMBURG

E. PRUSSIA

17 Sept 1939 Russia invades Poland

KHARKOV

LONDON

BERLIN

Vistula

WARSAW

KIEV

Dnieper

Don

Caspian Sea

DUNKIRK
BRUSSELS BELG.

COLOGNE

G E R M A N Y

POLAND

ROSTOV

10 May 1940 Germany invades the Low Countries and France

4 June 1940

Rhine

LUX.

PRAGUE

LVOV

ODESSA

SEVASTOPOL

TIFLIS

PARIS

Danube

SLOVAKIA

Bay of Biscay

VICHY

BERNE

SWITZ.

MUNICH

VIENNA

BUDAPEST

3

1

FRANCE

25 June 1940 BORDEAUX (Vichy France)

MILAN

HUNGARY

RUMANIA

BUCHAREST

BLACK SEA

MARSEILLES

TURIN

VENICE

BELGRADE

Danube

2

LISBON

MADRID

10 June 1940 Italy declares war on Britain and France

FLORENCE

YUGOSLAVIA

BULGARIA

IRAN

PORTUGAL

SPAIN

I T A L Y

ROME

Adriatic Sea

SOFIA

ANKARA

ISTANBUL

T U R K E Y

NAPLES

ALBANIA

Sardinia

GREECE

28 Oct 1940 Italy invades Greece

ATHENS

SYRIA (Fr)

IRAQ (Br)

GIBRALTAR (Br)
SP. MOR.

ORAN

PALERMO
Sicily

M E D I T E R R A N E A N

TUNIS

MALTA (Br)

Dodecanese (Italian)

Cyprus (Br)

DAMASCUS

CASABLANCA

ALGIERS

Crete

MOROCCO (Fr)

ALGERIA (Fr)

TUNISIA (Fr)

S E A

PALESTINE (Br)
JERUSALEM

AMMAN
TRANSJORDAN (Br)

TRIPOLI

TOBRUK

ALEXANDRIA

Suez Canal

SAUDI ARABIA

Ceded Rumanian territories :
1. Bessarabia & N. Bukovina to Russia, June 1940
2. S. Dobruja to Bulgaria, August 1940
3. Transylvania to Hungary, September 1940

SIRTE

BENGHAZI

EL AGHEILA

L I B Y A (Italian)

Nile

CAIRO

EGYPT (Br protectorate)

© Richard Natkiel, 1982

armies in both Greece and North Africa were struggling before the end of 1940. By that time, German U-boats were taking a heavy toll of Allied shipping on the convoy routes.

Above left: Saluting the Swastika.
Left: Axis expansion in the late 1930s.
Above: German and Italian territorial gains in 1939 and 1940.
Right: The dreaded Ju 87 Stuka dive bomber, whose success in Europe became legendary.

German Conquest at Its Height

Below: 1942 saw the high tidemark of German expansion. Allied landings in North Africa combined with the Soviet counteroffensive on the Eastern Front were to turn the tide and sound the death-knell for Hitler's territorial aspirations.

Having been balked in his plan to invade the British Isles, Hitler directed his attention to the east, where he gained control of the Balkans in the spring of 1941. He shored up the tenuous Italian position in North Africa, then ordered the implementation of Operation Barbarossa – the invasion of the Soviet Union. Operations beginning 22 June 1941 inflicted great losses on the Red Army, but the expected quick and easy victory was not forthcoming. German confidence and supplies began to erode with the onset of an early winter that found troops unequipped for freezing conditions. The Russian Bear shook off its tormentors in a counteroffensive that prevented the capture of Moscow, then Stalingrad, in 1942. Russian civilians proved able defenders of their embattled homeland, and the Germans went onto the defensive in Russia. An ill-advised declaration of war on the United States after Pearl Harbor guaranteed open and active American involvement, with all the industrial and military strength that this implied. Hitler's Germany had overreached itself.

The Propaganda War

Propaganda was used by all of the belligerents in World War II to incite patriotism and inflame popular feeling against 'the enemy,' both outside and within the country. Luridly illustrated Soviet posters trumpeted 'Kill the German Beasts!' and 'Destroy the Hitlerite Army – It can and must be done!' Soviet leaders did not feel fully confident of their peoples' loyalty in every phase of the war, in which they lost more soldiers and civilians than any other single belligerent.

Germany produced comparable war art from 1943 on, after the office of National Socialist Leadership was created. Psychological warfare played a major role in the German war effort, with the production of films, posters, magazines and other media that fostered unquestioning loyalty and hatred of minorities, who were accused of subverting the war effort. During World War I, propaganda had been so falsified by all parties involved that genuine atrocities like 'The Final Solution to the Jewish Problem' were widely disbelieved – until Allied liberation of concentration camp survivors in 1945 revealed the incredible truth.

The US propaganda effort was less obvious, but not necessarily less effective. Marine recruitment posters bore the legend: 'We're looking for a few good men,' emphasizing the Marines' reputation as an élite force. 'War Bonds' and 'Victory Gardens' abounded to foster wholehearted co-operation on the home front. 'Remember Pearl Harbor' was taken up as a powerful rallying cry in the war against Japan. Thus dictatorships and democracies alike waged the propaganda war with deep intensity and unshakeable conviction of the rightness of their cause.

Below: Japan's sphere of influence and activity, December 1941.
Below right: Soldiers return to Japan from Manchuria to a hero's welcome.

1931
'The Mukden incident'
Japan overruns
Manchuria

1933
Japan annexes
Jehol

7 July 1937
Japan invades
China

27 September 1940
Japan signs 'Tripartite'
pact with Germany and
Italy, and in April 1941,
a non-aggression pact
with Russia

August 1940
Japan establishes
military bases in
French Indo-China
and in July 1941,
occupies the country

RUSSIA

ATTU

ULAN BATOR

MONGOLIA

Sakhalin

Kurile Is

ETEROFU
Hitokappu B

MANCHURIA
HARBIN
(MANCHUKUO)

VLADIVOSTOK

Hokkaido

Jehol

MUKDEN

SEA OF
JAPAN

PEKING

KOREA

SEOUL

Honshu

C H I N A

TSINGTAO

NAGASAKI

TOKYO

JAPAN

Hwang Ho

NANKING
HANKOW

Shikoku
Kyushu

Kagoshima B

SHANGHAI

DELHI

CHUNGKING Kiang

Yangtze

CHANGSHA

Burma Road

Ryukyu Is

OKINAWA

BONIN IS

P   A   C

NEPAL

Ganges

IMPHAL

KUNMING

CANTON

Formosa
(Taiwan)

IWO JIMA

MARCUS

C

CALCUTTA

LASHIO

MANDALAY

HONG KONG

HAINAN

Luzon

WAKE

I N D I A

BOMBAY

BURMA

HANOI

HAIPHONG

Mariana
Islands

SAIPAN

O

C   E

RANGOON

THAI-
LAND

FRENCH
INDO-CHINA

PHILIPPINE
ISLANDS

GUAM

BAY OF BENGAL

BANGKOK

SAIGON

MANILA

LEYTE

ENIWETOK

KWAJALEIN

MADRAS

ANDAMAN
IS

SOUTH CHINA
SEA

Mindanao

YAP

TRUK

Marshall
Is

TRINCOMALEE

NICOBAR
IS

KOTA BHARU

DAVAO

PALAU IS

C a r o l i n e   I s l a n d s

MAJURO

MAKIN

COLOMBO

Ceylon

Str of Malacca

MALAYA

N BORNEO

SARAWAK

Molucca Passage

TARAWA

Equator

SINGAPORE

HALMAHERA

Gilbert Is

ADDU
ATOLL

Sumatra

Borneo

Celebes

Makassar Str

New Guinea

ADMIRALTY
IS

NEW
BRITAIN

NEW IRELAND

RABAUL

NAURU

OCEAN I

DUTCH   EAST   INDIES

BATAVIA

Java

FLORES

TIMOR

PAPUA

BOUGAINVILLE

NEW
GEORGIA

Solomon Is

GUADALCANAL

COCOS IS

ARAFURA SEA

PORT
MORESBY

GUADALCANAL

SANTA CRUZ
IS

I N D I A N   O C E A N

TIMOR SEA

DARWIN

CORAL SEA

CAIRNS

ESPIRITU
SANTO

New
Hebrides

EFATE

New
Caledonia

NOUMEA

Northern
Territory

Queensland

ROCKHAMPTON

Western
Australia

A U S T R A L I A

South
Australia

BRISBANE

NORFOLK

PERTH

New
South Wales

SYDNEY

ADELAIDE

CANBERRA

Victoria

MELBOURNE

AUCKLAND

JAPANESE EMPIRE, 1933

OCCUPIED BY JAPAN,
7 JULY 1937 – 7 DEC 1941

AREA UNDER JAPANESE CONTROL
7 DECEMBER 1941

MERCATOR'S PROJECTION

Japan Asserts Its Power

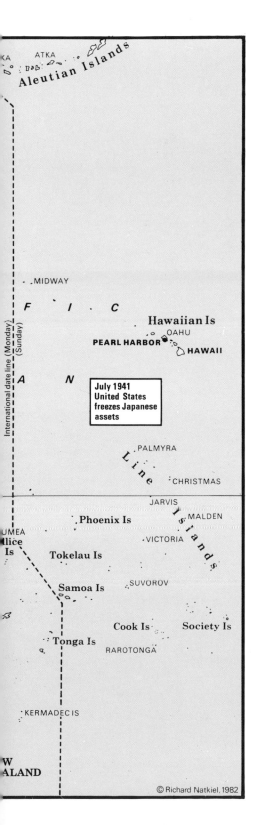

Japanese resentment at the Pacific settlement following World War I gathered strength through the 1920s. 'Patriotic Societies' agitated for an aggressive foreign policy, and the Japanese constitution gave the military a disproportionate voice in national affairs. The rise of Chinese Nationalism posed a threat to Japan's position as the leading Asian power, and the West was widely distrusted as racist in its attitudes – not without cause.

All these factors were involved in the Japanese seizure of Manchuria (1931), which was made by the so-called Japanese Manchurian Army acting independently of the government. Two years later, Japan withdrew from the League of Nations and accelerated her arms production. Serious fighting with China broke out in 1937 and resulted in Japanese occupation of most major Chinese ports and extensive areas of their territory.

To prevent the Chinese from being supplied through French Indochina, the Japanese put pressure on the area and ended by occupying it in 1941. This brought open opposition from the US in the form of an export embargo. Japan's recent pacts with the Axis Powers and the USSR had imperiled Allied interests in the Pacific, and stringent sanctions against Japanese trade and oil imports were decisive. Faced with the loss of 75 percent of her trade and 90 percent of her oil supplies, Japan sent her aircraft carrier force into the Pacific on 26 November 1941. On 2 December General Tojo, now militant Prime Minister of Japan, ordered it to attack the US Pacific Fleet at Pearl Harbor, Hawaii.

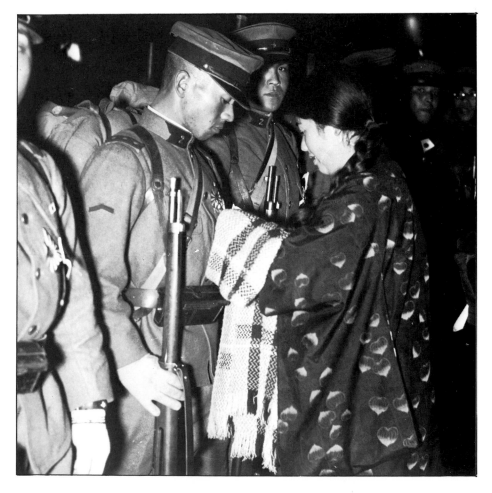

Below right: Japan's surprise attack at Pearl Harbor, Hawaii, on 7 December 1941 (below) raised the curtain on nine months of feverish expansion in the Pacific – yet the scale of this empire-building was destined to sap her strength.

RUSSIA

ULAN BATOR

MONGOLIA

Sakhalin

ATTU

6-7 June 1942
Attu & Kiska
occupied

Kurile Is

MANCHURIA

HARBIN
(MANCHUKUO)

ETEROFU

Hitokappu B

VLADIVOSTOK

Hokkaido

MUKDEN

PEKING

KOREA

SEOUL

SEA OF JAPAN

Honshu

C H I N A

TSINGTAO

NAGASAKI

Shikoku

TOKYO

JAPAN

6 August 1942
Limit of Japanese
expansion

15 Jan-15 May 1942
Invasion of Burma

CHUNGKING

Yangtze-kiang

NANKING

HANKOW

SHANGHAI

Kyushu

Kagoshima B

BONIN IS

P

A

C

DELHI

NEPAL

Ganges

IMPHAL

CHANGSHA

Burma Road

KUNMING

CANTON

Ryukyu Is

OKINAWA

IWO JIMA

MARCUS

O

C

CALCUTTA

LASHIO

MANDALAY

HANOI

HAIPHONG

HONG KONG

Formosa
(Taiwan)

8-25 December 1941
Invasion of Hong Kong

WAKE

I N D I A

BURMA

HAINAN

Luzon

Mariana
Islands

SAIPAN

GUAM

ENIWETOK

KWAJALEIN

BOMBAY

RANGOON

BAY OF BENGAL

THAI-
LAND

FRENCH
INDO-CHINA

MANILA

PHILIPPINE
ISLANDS

LEYTE

8 December 1941
Philippines invaded.
Surrendered
6 May 1942

TRUK

Marshall
Is

MAJURO

MADRAS

ANDAMAN
IS

BANGKOK

SAIGON

SOUTH CHINA
SEA

Mindanao

Davao

Caroline Islands

MAKIN

TARAWA

TRINCOMALEE

NICOBAR
IS

KOTA BHARU

N BORNEO

Molucca Passage

COLOMBO

Ceylon

Str of Malacca

MALAYA

SARAWAK

HALMAHERA

Makassar Str

23 Jan-1 August 1942
Solomon Islands, NE New
Guinea and part of Papua
captured

Equator

SINGAPORE

Borneo

Celebes

ADMIRALTY
IS

NEW
IRELAND

ADDU
ATOLL

8 December 1941
Thailand occupied

Sumatra

DUTCH   **EAST INDIES**

New Guinea

NEW
BRITAIN

RABAUL

BOUGAINVILLE

Solomon Is

8 December 1941
Malaya invaded.
15 February 1942
Singapore falls

BATAVIA

Java

FLORES

TIMOR

PAPUA

NEW
GEORGIA

GUADALCANAL

11 Jan-8 March 1942
Invasion of Dutch
East Indies

ARAFURA SEA

PORT
MORESBY

SANTA CRUZ
IS

COCOS IS

TIMOR SEA

DARWIN

CORAL SEA

ESPIRITU
SANTO

New
Hebrides

EFATE

I N D I A N   O C E A N

Northern
Territory

Queensland

CAIRNS

4-8 May 1942
Battle of Coral Sea

New
Caledonia

NOUMEA

Western
Australia

ROCKHAMPTON

NORFOLK

AUSTRALIA

PERTH

South
Australia

New
South Wales

BRISBANE

ADELAIDE

Victoria

MELBOURNE

SYDNEY

CANBERRA

AUCKLAND

JAPANESE CONTROLLED AT
7 DECEMBER 1941
OCCUPIED BY JAPAN,
7 DECEMBER 1941 – 6 AUGUST 1942

MERCATOR'S PROJECTION

The Japanese Sweep the Pacific

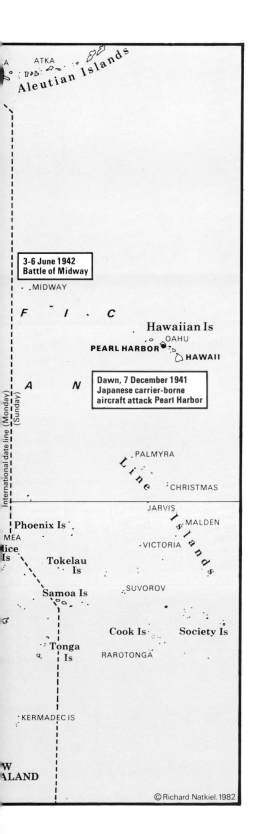

3-6 June 1942
Battle of Midway

· MIDWAY

F   I   C

Hawaiian Is
○ OAHU
PEARL HARBOR 🏝 △ HAWAII

Dawn, 7 December 1941
Japanese carrier-borne
aircraft attack Pearl Harbor

A   N

· PALMYRA
· CHRISTMAS
JARVIS
Phoenix Is · · MALDEN
· VICTORIA
Tokelau Is
· SUVOROV
Samoa Is
Cook Is · Society Is
· Tonga Is
RAROTONGA

· KERMADEC IS

W ALAND

© Richard Natkiel. 1982

When the Japanese aimed their stunning strike at Pearl Harbor, their strategists expected – and achieved – a series of rapid victories in the Pacific. They had no real choice: without access to oil, their war machine would grind to a halt even as US industry geared up for new feats of production under wartime conditions. The oil-rich East Indies were an inevitable target, as were the Allied colonies astride the sea routes.

Available forces were relatively modest – some 80 percent of the 51 Japanese divisions were tied up in China and Manchuria. On the plus side, the outnumbered Japanese troops had good air support, jungle-warfare training and an impressive fleet that included 10 carriers and 8 modern battleships. (The US Pacific Fleet had nine battleships of World War I vintage and four carriers that – fortunately – were absent from Pearl Harbor when the initial attack was launched.) Japanese Imperial Headquarters believed it was possible to achieve their objectives within six months if they moved decisively, and for the first four months they effectively had the Pacific War to themselves.

At a cost of only 23 warships (none larger than a destroyer), the Japanese overran the Philippines, Malaya, Burma, the Dutch East Indies and a number of British islands between December 1941 and May 1942. Then the Doolittle Raid on Tokyo (18 April) awakened them to the danger of bombing on the home islands, and inflamed the Japanese 'Victory Disease' (as one of their leaders would call it). The Japanese resolved to extend their defense perimeter despite their diminishing resources – and thereby ensured that they would lose the war.

Below: Japan's empire-building was finally curtailed as a two-pronged Allied offensive from the east and southwest forced a retreat.
Below right: US and British combined chiefs of staff discuss Allied strategy.

RUSSIA

ULAN BATOR

MONGOLIA

MANCHURIA
(MANCHUKUO)
HARBIN

MUKDEN

VLADIVOSTOK

PEKING

KOREA

SEOUL

C H I N A

SEA OF JAPAN

Sakhalin

Kurile Is

ETEROFU
Hitokappu B

Hokkaido

ATTU

15 Aug 1943

7 March–22 June 1944
Japanese invasion of N-E India repulsed

TSINGTAO

NANKING

HANKOW

SHANGHAI

CHUNGKING

CHANGSHA

Burma Road

Honshu

TOKYO
JAPAN

NAGASAKI

Shikoku
Kyushu
Kagoshima B

Ryukyu Is

OKINAWA

BONIN IS

IWO JIMA

P A C I

MARCUS

WAKE

Hwang Ho

Yangtze kiang

DELHI

NEPAL

Ganges

IMPHAL

KUNMING

CANTON

Formosa
(Taiwan)

HONG KONG

Mariana
Islands

SAIPAN

15 June 1944

18 Feb 1944

31 Jan 1944

KWAJALEIN

CALCUTTA

LASHIO
MANDALAY

HANOI

HAIPHONG

HAINAN

Luzon

GUAM

ENIWETOK

21 July 1944

TRUK

Marshall
Is

MAJURO

MAKIN

TARAWA

I N D I A

BOMBAY

BURMA

RANGOON

THAI-
LAND

BANGKOK

FRENCH
INDO-CHINA

SAIGON

MANILA

PHILIPPINE
ISLANDS

LEYTE

Mindanao

DAVAO

YAP

PALAU IS

O

C

Caroline Islands

Gilbert Is

MADRAS

ANDAMAN
IS

TRINCOMALEE

COLOMBO

Ceylon

NICOBAR
IS

KOTA BHARU

SOUTH CHINA
SEA

N BORNEO

SARAWAK

Molucca Passage

Makassar Str

Str of Malacca

MALAYA

SINGAPORE

Borneo

HALMAHERA

ADMIRALTY
IS

26 Dec 1943

NAURU

1 Nov 1944

OCEAN

Sumatra

Celebes

D U T C H   E A S T   I N D I E S

BATAVIA

Java

FLORES

New Guinea

NEW
IRELAND

NEW
BRITAIN

RABAUL

BOUGAINVILLE

Solomon Is

GUADALCANAL

SANTA CRUZ
IS

South East Asia
Command
(Mountbatten)

ADDU
ATOLL

Equator

I N D I A N   O C E A N

COCOS IS

TIMOR

PAPUA

PORT
MORESBY

NEW
GEORGIA

7 Aug 1942

CORAL SEA

ESPIRITU
SANTO

New
Hebrides

EFATE

ARAFURA SEA

TIMOR SEA

DARWIN

30 June 1943

New
Caledonia

NOUMEA

Aug 1942–July 1944
US/Australian landings along north coast of New Guinea

South-West
Pacific Area
(MacArthur)

Western
Australia

Queensland

ROCKHAMPTON

NORFOLK

A U S T R A L I A

South
Australia

BRISBANE

New
South Wales

PERTH

ADELAIDE

Victoria

MELBOURNE

New
South Wales

SYDNEY
CANBERRA

AUCKLAND

———	ALLIED COMMAND BOUNDARIES, 2 JULY 1942	
– – –	SUBDIVISIONS OF PACIFIC OCEAN AREAS	
▬▬▬	LIMIT OF JAPANESE EXPANSION, 6 AUGUST 1942	
▨	AREA REOCCUPIED BY AMERICAN FORCES, 6 AUGUST 1942 – AUG 1944	
1 Nov 1944	DATES OF MAIN AMERICAN LANDINGS	
☐	AREA OCCUPIED BY JAPANESE FORCES, JUNE–AUGUST 1944	

MERCATOR'S PROJECTION

The Allies Strike Back at Japan

North Pacific Area (Nimitz)

Pacific Ocean Areas (Nimitz)

Central Pacific Area (Kinkaid)

South Pacific Area (Ghormley, Halsey later)

20 Nov 1943

Aleutian Islands

ATKA

MIDWAY

Hawaiian Is

OAHU

PEARL HARBOR

HAWAII

PALMYRA

CHRISTMAS

JARVIS

Phoenix Is

MALDEN

VICTORIA

Tokelau Is

Samoa Is

SUVOROV

Cook Is

Society Is

Tonga Is

RAROTONGA

KERMADEC IS

Line Islands

© Richard Natkiel. 1982

As US forces gained experience in the challenging Pacific Theater, their leaders saw the necessity for mounting two major lines of advance against Japan. US Navy carrier forces were strengthened for their essential role, amphibious assault capability was increased and a fleet train was created to supply the fighting ships hundreds of miles from their bases. These units were to advance toward Japan via the central Pacific islands. Test case for the 'island-hopping' strategy was Tarawa, where US forces fought one of the costliest battles in their history in proportion to the numbers engaged in November 1943. Three thousand US Marines were casualties, and only 17 of the 4000 Japanese defenders were captured. An intensive study of this campaign helped the Americans to avoid their mistakes on Tarawa in subsequent operations. They accepted the fact that the Japanese would have to be flushed out of their caves and bunkers one by one, using grenades, flamethrowers and anything else that came to hand.

The other half of the Allied offensive was in the southwest Pacific, where American and Australian forces under General Douglas MacArthur made slow but certain progress with massive support from land-based aircraft. Australian forces had a strong vested interest in defeating the Japanese, who were sure to attack their homeland if they could isolate it from American support.

The Defeat of Nazi Germany

Germany's long retreat began in 1943; the Battle of Kursk in July of that year was the death knell for hopes of victory in the east. Two months before, Italy had been knocked out of the war, and it was only a matter of time before the Allies would try to break into Fortress Europe. The German threat to the Atlantic supply routes was effectively nullified, and before the year was out, US and British bombers were attacking both industrial targets and population centers within the Reich.

By the middle of 1944, after successful massive Allied landings in Normandy and breakthroughs aimed at the Rhine, the combined might of US and Soviet industry and armies had become overwhelming. British resources were strained, but not to the breaking point. In fact, Allied organization and equipment were at their peak. The Germans, by contrast, were drained in every area: men, money, armaments and leadership. By the time Allied forces converged on the Elbe to link up with the Russians (April-May 1945), most German units were prepared to show the white flag. Town after town surrendered eagerly to the Allies in preference to the feared Russians.

© Richard Natkiel, 1982

Below left: The contraction and (below) final defeat of Hitler's Germany.
Right: Berlin lies in ruins, the target of round-the-clock raids by British and US bomber aircraft.

94

Below: The reversal of Japanese supremacy in the Pacific was confirmed by the Allies' recapture of the Philippines in early 1945. Defeat was then only a matter of months away.
Below right: A postwar view of the business district of Kobe, showing the damage caused by incendiary attack.

Dissolution of the Japanese Empire

The first real check to the Japanese came with the Battle of the Coral Sea, six months after Pearl Harbor. There US carriers commanded by Rear Admiral Frank 'Black-Jack' Fletcher dashed Japanese hopes of capturing Port Moresby, the key to New Guinea. The battle made history as the first naval engagement in which opposing ships never sighted each other – all fighting was done by carrier-based planes. Both sides made serious errors in this new form of warfare, but many of these were corrected by US forces in the subsequent Battle of Midway.

In this action, the island of Midway served as an 'unsinkable aircraft carrier' for Admiral Chester W Nimitz. Bungled Japanese intelligence contributed to a disaster from which the Japanese Navy would not recover – the loss of every carrier commanded by Admiral Chuichi Nagumo. After Midway, the Japanese would be incapable of supporting the far-flung conquests so rapidly made in preceding months.

To preclude a second Japanese attempt on Port Moresby, the Americans determined to seize Tulagi and Guadalcanal in the Solomon Islands. It was a six-month struggle in which US forces gained additional skills from day to day despite heavy losses, and it set the tone for the duration of the Pacific War – a campaign that moved steadily toward Japan by avoiding heavily garrisoned enemy strongholds and seizing weaker positions to use as a springboard to the next American objective.

General Matsuichi Ino summarized after the war: 'The Americans attacked and seized, with minimum losses, a relatively weak area, constructed airfields, and then proceeded to cut supply lines . . . Our strongpoints were gradually starved out.' It was a brilliant improvisation on the theme of the indirect approach.

The Japanese Juggernaut

RUSSIA

Kamchatka

ATTU

ULAN BATOR ■

MONGOLIA

MANCHURIA
HARBIN
(MANCHUKUO)

Sakhalin

Kurile Is

26 Nov 1941
Nagumo's fleet
sails

4 Dec
Refue
point

ETOROFU

Tankan Bay

VLADIVOSTOK

MUKDEN

Hokkaido

PEKING

C H I N A

Hwang Ho

KOREA

SEOUL

SEA OF
JAPAN

Honshu

TOKYO
JAPAN

7 Dec 1941

16 Dec
Part of fleet
to Wake I. in
support of atta

NANKING
HANKOW

NAGASAKI
KAGOSHIMA

Shikoku
Kyushu

Shanghai

DELHI ■

NEPAL

CHUNGKING

Yangtse-kiang

Ganges

CHANGSHA

Burma Road

KARACHI

IMPHAL

KUNMING

LASHIO

Ryukyu Is

BONIN IS

IWO JIMA

P A C I

KALCUTTA

CALCUTTA

MANDALAY

CANTON

PESCADORES
IS

Formosa
(Taiwan)

8 Dec
Wake I. attacked
23 Dec
surrendered

WAKE (USA)

I N D I A

BURMA

HANOI

HONG KONG
(Brit.)

O

C E

Marianas
Islands

BOMBAY

RANGOON

THAI-
LAND

BANGKOK

FRENCH
INDO-CHINA

HAINAN

SAIGON

MANILA

Luzon

PHILIPPINE
ISLANDS

SAIPAN

GUAM (USA)

ENIWETOK

KWAJALEIN

Marsha
Islands

MAJUR

BAY OF
BENGAL

MADRAS

ANDAMAN
IS

SOUTH CHINA
SEA

Mindanao

YAP

TRUK

MAKIN

TRINCOMALEE

NICOBAR
IS

KHOTA BHARU

DAVAO

PALAU IS

Caroline   Islands

TARAWA

Gilb
Is

COLOMBO

Ceylon

N BORNEO

Maldive
Is

Equator

MALAYA

SARAWAK

NAURU

OCEAN I

SINGAPORE

Borneo

Sumatra

DUTCH   EAST   INDIES

Celebes

HALMAHERA

NEW
IRELAND

NEW
BRITAIN   RABAUL

NANUMEA

BATAVIA

Java

FLORES

New Guinea

PAPUA

BOUGAINVILLE

Solomon Is

Ellice
Is

I N D I A N

TIMOR

ARAFURA SEA

PORT
MORESBY

NEW
GEORGIA   GUADALCANAL

SANTA
CRUZ IS

ESPIRITU-SANTO

TIMOR SEA

DARWIN

CORAL SEA

CAIRNS

New
Hebrides

EFATE

Fi
Is

SU

O C E A N

Northern
Territory

New
Caledonia

NOUMEA

A U S T R A L I A

Western
Australia

Queensland

ROCKHAMPTON

NORFOLK

South
Australia

New South
Wales

BRISBANE

PERTH

ADELAIDE

Victoria

SYDNEY
CANBERRA

TASMAN

AUCKLAND

MELBOURNE

SEA

WELLINGTON

NEW ZEALAND

CHRISTCHURCH

JAPANESE EMPIRE, 1933
OCCUPIED BY JAPAN, JULY 1937/DECEMBER 1941
MILITARY BASES ESTABLISHED BY JAPAN, SEPTEMBER 1940
ABDA (American, British, Dutch, and Australian) COMMAND
MERCATOR'S PROJECTION

Previous page: The battleship Yamato
fitting out at Kure, Japan, in 1941.
Above: Japan's occupied territories.
Right and far right: The Pearl Harbor
attacks in detail.
Above right: The magazine of the US
destroyer Shaw *explodes during the raids.*

Pearl Harbor

The Japanese strike force that approached Pearl Harbor on 6 December consisted of six fleet carriers escorted by two battleships and two heavy cruisers. Anchored in Pearl Harbor were eight battleships of the US Pacific Fleet, numerous destroyers and tenders, and submarines and minesweepers. The carriers *Lexington* and *Saratoga* were away on a supply mission to Wake Island, which was fortunate for the future course of the war on the Allied side.

Radio monitoring of increased Japanese radio traffic in the several days preceding the attack made it clear that an operation was underway. All Pacific forces had been alerted, but those at Pearl Harbor remained on a peacetime footing despite the danger. Aircraft on the several Oahu airfields were undispersed, and ships were anchored in line with many members of their crews ashore. Reconnaissance flights had not been increased above the average.

Pearl Harbor

FIRST ATTACK BY TORPEDO-BOMBERS

The Japanese launched the first wave of their two-part air attack at 6:00 AM on 7 December. A radar station reported incoming planes at 7:00 AM, but this report was unaccountably ignored. An hour later, torpedo bombers came in to attack the harbor as fighters began to strafe the airfields. Virtually all the US aircraft were destroyed on the ground. In the harbor, five of the eight battleships were hit immediately; minutes later, *West Virginia* was in flames and sinking, *Oklahoma* had capsized and *California* was badly damaged. *Arizona* had exploded and *Nevada* had to beach herself as she made for the harbor entrance under fire from the second wave of the Japanese attack. Dive bombers and high-level bombers had joined the first aircraft contingent to create additional devastation.

By the time the second wave struck, US forces had rallied from the initial shock to offer a more effective defense. At 9:45 AM, Vice-Admiral Nagumo's aircraft returned to their carriers with loss of nine fighters, fifteen dive bombers and five torpedo bombers.

Had Admiral Nagumo launched an additional attack against the harbor, he might have destroyed the port facilities entirely and accounted for the absent aircraft carriers as well. Instead, he chose to withdraw the strike force, from which he dispatched several units to attack Wake Island (8 December). US Marines garrisoned there sank two Japanese destroyers and held the island against steady air and sea bombardment for two weeks, until they were overwhelmed by a Japanese landing.

Malaya

Lieutenant General Tomoyuki Yamashita commanded the Japanese Twenty-fifth Army in its whirlwind invasion of Malaya (December 1941). In this campaign, which drove all the way to Singapore and was described by Winston Churchill as the worst disaster in British military history, Yamashita earned the nickname 'Tiger of Malaya.' His force consisted of three divisions supported by 600 aircraft, as against Lieutenant General A E Percival's two divisions with some 150 aircraft.

Northern landings met little opposition except at Kota Bharu, where Takumi Force, a regimental group, had to fight its way ashore. Meanwhile, air attacks wiped out all but some 50 British planes.

A double advance south was led by the Japanese 5 Division, which grappled with 11 Indian Division around Jitra on 11 December. The defenders were pushed back steadily, as the Japanese Guards Division moved down the coast and 5 and 18 Divisions progressed inland. Within 70 days, Yamashita's troops had overrun all of Malaya through a combination of superior force, speed and surprise. General Percival was tricked by skillful jungle-warfare tactics into believing that the Japanese force was vastly superior in size, and on 15 February 1942 he and his men surrendered.

Above left: Aftermath of Pearl Harbor, with USS Downes *at left, USS* Cassin *at right and USS* Pennsylvania *at rear.*
Left: The garrison flag flies as Hickam Field burns.
Right: The Japanese conquest of Malaya, completed in January 1942.
Below right: Singapore falls in February.
Below: General Yamashita (foreground) surveys newly-conquered territory.

The Fall of Hong Kong

Simultaneous with the Japanese invasion of the Malay Peninsula on 8 December 1941 came the invasion of Hong Kong, whose defenders were hopelessly outnumbered. Within 24 hours they had been pushed back to the Gindrinkers Line, which was breached by the capture of Shing Mun Redoubt. The mainland then had to be evacuated, an operation which was completed on 13 December. Five days later the Japanese crossed Kowloon Bay on a wide front and captured more than half of Hong Kong Island. Fierce resistance continued until several days before Christmas, but after most of the reservoirs were captured, the garrison was forced to surrender on 25 December.

Above: British soldiers face captivity after the fall of Hong Kong.
Right: Hong Kong and the surrounding area.

Above: The Japanese take Hong Kong on Christmas Day 1941.
Opposite top: The Japanese conquest of Bataan, completed in April 1942.
Opposite: The last US forces to hold out on Corregidor Island, south of Bataan, were finally neutralized on the morning of 6 May.

Victory in the Philippines

In July 1941, when the Philippine Army joined forces with the United States, General Douglas MacArthur was made commander of US Forces in the Far East (USAFFE). His ten divisions included some 19,000 American troops and 160,000 Filipinos – most of them ill equipped and undertrained. There were also 200 aircraft at his disposal. The Japanese believed, with some justification, that their Fourteenth Army of two divisions supported by 500 aircraft could conquer the Philippine Islands.

Heavy air attacks struck US air bases on 8 December (the same day as Pearl Harbor, but dated a day later by the International Date Line). Word of the Pearl Harbor disaster had impelled USAFFE to fly its bombers off Clark Field in the morning, but by the time of the midday attack, they were back on the ground with their fighter escorts. Forty-eight hours of bombing against the airfields accounted for the vast majority of US warplanes and cleared the way for Japanese landings north of Luzon to seize the bases at Vigan, Laoag and Tuguegarao. In the south, Legaspi was seized as a base from which to interdict seaborne US reinforcements.

The main Japanese landings were at Lingayen Bay on 22 December, whence the invaders broke out of their beachhead to advance against Manila. On 23 December MacArthur announced his plan to withdraw to Bataan; five days later, he declared Manila an open city. By early January, the Japanese were gaining ground on the Bataan Peninsula, but their troops were overtaken by disease there and gained little ground for the next two months.

On 12 March 1942, MacArthur was flown out and replaced by Lieutenant General Jonathan Wainwright, who frustrated several Japanese attempts to establish beachheads behind US lines. Not until 3 April, after reinforcement by a fresh division, were the Japanese able to launch their final offensive. Within a week's time, they had penetrated so deeply that US forces were compelled to surrender (7 April). The last American troops held out on Corregidor Island in a siege that ran from January until 5 May, when their artillery was almost entirely knocked out by unceasing bombardments. On that day, Japanese troops landed at Cavalry Point and established their beachhead. It was all over for the time being in the Philippines.

Left: Japanese landings on Luzon, December 1941.
Above: Small Japanese field gun in action during the Bataan campaign, April 1942.
Right: American prisoners of war under guard by Japanese troops after the surrender of Bataan.

The Dutch East Indies

The oil and other resources of the Dutch East Indies made them a prime target for occupation by Japan, which planned a three-part attack on the islands early in 1942. Western Force, from Indochina and newly captured Sarawak, would attack southern Sumatra, Western Java, and North Borneo; Central Force would attack Borneo from Davao; and Eastern Force would jump off from the same point against the Celebes, Amboina, Timor, Bali and eastern Java.

Defense of the islands was undertaken by a combined force of Allies in the Southwest Pacific: American, British, Dutch and Australian (ABDA). General Archibald Wavell and his forces had more courage than support, which consisted largely of a six-cruiser naval flotilla under Dutch Rear Admiral Karel Doorman. The attacks began on 11 January 1942, and proceeded relentlessly from one objective to another in the weeks that followed. Naval engagements off Balikpapan (24 January) and in the Lombok Straits (19-20 February) provided only a slight check to the Japanese advance. On 27 February Admiral Doorman attacked the Eastern

Force convoy in the Java Sea, where both Dutch cruisers were sunk before they could inflict any damage. In the aftermath, HMS *Exeter* was also destroyed, as were HMAS *Perth* and USS *Houston* when they resisted the Western Force on the following day – to some effect in terms of damage done. But on 1 March, the Japanese made their inevitable landing on Java, whose Allied defenders succumbed a week later.

Above: Japan captures the East Indies piecemeal, 1942.
Right: A Japanese column in Burma crosses a footbridge south of Moulmein.
Far right: The invasion of Burma was accomplished with little Allied resistance.

Burma Bows to Japan

The Japanese invasion of Burma began on 15 January 1942 with the occupation of Victoria Point by a detachment of Fifteenth Army, which moved north to take Tavoy four days later. British defenses in Burma were pathetically unprepared to resist the Japanese invaders; only two brigades, one Indian and one Burmese, were able to counter the push toward Moulmein that began on 20 January. The British were then forced back from the town under constant threat of being outflanked, and from this point on fought a series of delaying actions all the way to Rangoon – the conduit for all British supplies and reinforcements. Air support from a single RAF squadron and a squadron of Major Claire Chennault's 'Flying Tigers' was insufficient to prevent the capture of Rangoon on 8 March. The British garrison there was very nearly cut off before it could pull out. Meanwhile, Lieutenant General William Slim had taken command of British ground forces, while General Harold Alexander had assumed overall command of the deteriorating British defense. The Chinese Fifth and Sixth Armies arrived to reinforce the Allies, but they fought erratically despite the best efforts of American commander General Joseph Stilwell. Throughout the month of April, Allied forces were in continuous retreat from the Japanese, who were now bringing in reinforcements and air support from conquered Malaya. By mid May they were in control of Burma.

The Italian Campaign

The Conquest of Sicily

When the Tunisian bridgehead collapsed on 12 May 1943, a demoralized Italy found herself in imminent danger of invasion. Serious strikes in industrial northern Italy had already warned both Mussolini and Hitler of the depth of national discontent. In a meeting with Hitler on 7 April, Mussolini tried – and failed – to persuade his ally to forget about Russia and concentrate on Mediterranean defense. On 5 May General von Rintelin reported to Hitler that an Allied landing in Italy would probably have 'most unpleasant consequences, in view of the prevailing atmosphere of fatalism.' Hitler remained adamant about his doomed adventure on the Eastern Front, which would finally collapse in July at the Battle of Kursk.

Even as Russian and German tanks battered each other in the Kursk Salient, the Allies launched their invasion of Italy, which Churchill had described as 'the soft underbelly of the Axis.' Aerial bombardment from North Africa struck Axis airfields and communications centers in Sicily, Sardinia and southern Italy, beginning in early June. Land forces for the invasion comprised General George S Patton's US Seventh Army and General Bernard Montgomery's British Eighth Army; they were transported to Sicily in a fleet of 3000 vessels. Axis defense of Sicily was entrusted to the Italian Sixth Army under General Alfredo Guzzoni, with strong German support.

On 10 July the Americans landed in Sicily's Gulf of Gela, the British in the Gulf of Syracuse. The landings were a surprise to the Italians, coming as they did in poor weather that seemed to preclude air- or seaborne operations. Vigorous German counterattacks against the Americans came from German divisions on 11-12 July, but Patton's force pressed on toward the north coast, clearing western Sicily by 23 July. Montgomery suffered a check at Catania, but small amphibious operations allowed him to continue his advance to Messina, which he reached on 17 August. Meanwhile, the Italians, who had offered minimal resistance from the first, evacuated the island. The Germans were left to fight a rearguard campaign until the Allied victory of mid August.

The Peninsular Landings

On 24 July 1943, Mussolini was overthrown. His replacement, Marshal Ugo Cavallero, began secret armistice talks with the Allies. Hitler suspected that the Italians were trying to take themselves out of the war and sent German reinforcements into northern Italy to safeguard communications. Field Marshal Albert Kesselring advised him that an Allied landing in Italy could be expected soon after the conquest of Sicily – probably on the Gulf of Salerno near Naples.

On 3 September, the day that the armistice with Italy was signed, British Eighth Army made a landing on the toe of Italy, at Reggio di Calabria – largely as a diversion. The main landing did take place at Salerno, on 9 September, after the secret armistice with Italy was made public. General Mark Clark's US Fifth Army, with British X Corps, secured only four small beachheads in the face of a well-prepared German defense. Farther south, Montgomery was advancing through Calabria, and there had been a second British landing at Taranto.

From 9 through 14 September, the Fifth Army was in serious trouble at Salerno. German shells from the surrounding hills, followed by a powerful attack on the 12th, almost cut the Allies in half. Reinforcements arrived two days later, barely in time to salvage the operation, and by 18 September Clark's forces had consolidated the beachhead. When Montgomery's advance units arrived on 16 September, Kesselring began to withdraw north to the Gustav Line, which ran along the Rivers Garigliano and Sangro. The Allies pursued from both east and west until 8 October, when a rest halt was called on the Volturno/Termoli Line. The terrain grew increasingly rougher and the weather more severe as the Allied advance resumed in mid October.

Previous page: US troops liberate Rome, June 1944.
Left: Sicily falls to the Allies, 1943.
Above right: The main Allied landing in Italy was undertaken at Salerno by Clark's US Fifth Army.
Right: A diversionary attack at Reggio di Calabria by the British Eighth Army preceded the main attack, while a third landing was made at Taranto in the east.

Allied Drive on the Gustav Line

Fifth Army made a difficult crossing of the Volturno, swollen by autumn rains, beginning on 12 October 1943. The roadless mountains north of the river posed even greater obstacles. On the east coast, Eighth Army forced a passage over the Trigno River, but their progress on both sides of the central mountains was slowed by skillful German delaying tactics. Kesselring used the time gained to complete the impressive Gustav Line, which ran along the line of the Garigliano and Rapido Rivers, over the central mountains and north of the Sangro River to the Adriatic. German Tenth Army held the line under General Heinrich von Vietinghoff. The western end was especially strong, as it was backed by the mountains on either side of the Liri and by Cassino.

On 20 November US Fifth Army attacked this strong sector, at a very high cost in casualties. Painful progress brought Fifth Army almost as far as the Rapido, but there it was halted at year's end by arctic weather conditions. Montgomery had forced the Sangro on 15 November and broken through the line east of Lanciano. The British took Ortona on 27 December.

GERMAN DEFENCE POSITIONS
BARBARA LINE
BERNHARD (REINHARD) LINE
GUSTAV LINE

FRONT LINES
12 OCTOBER 1943
15 JANUARY 1944

MILES
0   15
KILOMETRES
0   25

Gran Sasso d'Italia

PENNE

PESCARA

90 Pz Gr Div

CHIETI

TOLLO

ORTONA
27 Dec

L'AQUILA

VILLA GRANDE
ROGATTI

SAN VITO

ARIELLI

1 Cdn Div   78 Div

POGGIOFIORITO

Pescara

ORSOGNA

FOSSACESIA
30 Nov

Rome Line

LANCIANO
5 Div

MOZZOGROGNA
28 Nov

20 Nov 1943
Eighth Army
crosses the Sangro

M Sirente

POPOLI

GUARDIAGRELE

2 NZ Div

65 Div

8 Ind Div

Adriatic Sea

LXXI Pz Corps
(Herr)

CASOLI

PERANO

VASTO
5 Nov

CELANO

M Amaro

1 Para Div

ARCHI

2 NZ Div

CASALANGUIDA

SAN SALVO

SULMONA

TORNARECCIO

16 Pz Div

TERMOLI

AVEZZANO

PALENA

29 Pz Gr Div

1 Para Div

Trigno

78 Div

To Rome

PALMOLI
5 Nov

Tenth Army
(Vietinghoff)

Liri

26 Pz Div

TORREBRUNA
5 Nov

MONTEFALCONE

Biferno

SERRACAPRIOLA

Br V Corps
(Allfrey;
Keightley later)

ROCCARASO

CASTIGLIONE
10 Nov

AGNONE

M Enerci

M Arazecca

BALSORANO

Castel di Sangro

TRIVENTO

8 Ind Div

LARINO

To Foggia

M Enerci

1 Cdn Div

CASACALENDA

ALFEDENA

5 Div

Fortore

SORA

S. DONATO
VAL DI COMINO

26 Pz Div
2 Mor Div

5 Div

Br XIII Corps
(Leese)

ARPINO

ATINA

Fr Exp Corps

COLLI

29 Pz Gr Div

CAMPOBASSO

ARCE

5 Mtn Div

3 Alg Div

ISERNIA
5 Nov

To Frosinone
& Rome

44 Div

US 34 Div

504
Para Bn

CANTALUPO
29 Oct

VINCHIATURO

RICCIA

Sacco

305 Div

Monte
Cassino

M Sammucro

1 Cdn Div

Rapido

CASSINO

VENAFRO
2 Nov

Eighth Army
(Montgomery)

3 Pz Gr Div

Route 6

Liri

SAN PIETRO

M Lungo

M Rotundo

US 45 Div

SAN BARTOLOMEO
IN GALDO

XIV Pz Corps
(Hube)

M Maggiore

MIGNANO   M Cesima

SANT'AMBROGIO

8
Dec

M Camino
6 Dec

PRESENZANO

FONDI

15 Pz Gr Div

M Petrella

M la Difensa
56 Div

US 3 Div

Volturno

PIEDIMONTE D'ALIFE

S. MARCO DEI CAVOTI

94 Div

Garigliano

M Sta
Croce

US 36 Div

26 Pz Div

MINTURNO

46 Div

DRAGONI

M Acero

US 45 Div

TEANO

GAETA

SESSA
AURUNCA

M Maggiore

AMOROSI

Raid by
commandos
Dec 1943

7 Armd Div

SPARANISE

CAIAZZO

SCHILLE

BENEVENTO

M Massico

Triflisco
Ridge

3 Pz Gr
Div

Calore

MONDRAGONE

Hermann
Göring
Pz Div

US 3 Div

US 34 Div

US VI Corps
(Lucas)

15 Oct

15 Pz
Gr Div

Volturno

CAPUA

CASERTA

Tyrrhenian Sea

GRAZZANISE

7 Armd Div   56 Div

CASTEL VOLTURNO
46 Div

13 Oct 1943
US Fifth Army
crosses the Volturno

Br X Corps
(McCreery)

US Fifth Army
(Clark)

Route 6

NAPLES

HEIGHT IN FEET
OVER 6000
3000-6000
1500-3000
600-1500
UNDER 600

Mt Vesuvius

To Salerno

The Fight for Monte Cassino

The ancient abbey of Monte Cassino astride the Gustav Line was the object of heavy fighting in the early months of 1944. The Allies made a frontal assault on the almost impregnable position on 17 January, but a whole series of attacks failed to take it by storm. The French Expeditionary Corps had joined the Allied forces in Italy, but they made only limited advances with very heavy casualties. The New Zealand Corps suffered similar repulses between 15 and 18 February.

A long hiatus followed the first offensive, during which the Allies regrouped and reinforced for a new effort, launched 11 May along a 20-mile front between the area east of Cassino and the sea. The British pushed over the Rapido but were then contained by the Germans. The Americans broke through the Gustav Line along the coast, only to be stopped at Santa Maria Infante. It was the French Expeditionary Force that crossed the Garigliano and cut the German lines of communication; interdiction of German supplies to the point of starvation was also a factor. On 17 May Kesselring conceded the loss of this key position by a withdrawal. The historic abbey had been riddled with tunnels and redoubts to protect its defenders from heavy bombardment; it was reduced to rubble by the time the Allies claimed it on 18 May, at the cost of many lives.

Right: Initial Allied attempts to break the Gustav Line at Cassino in early 1944 met with failure.

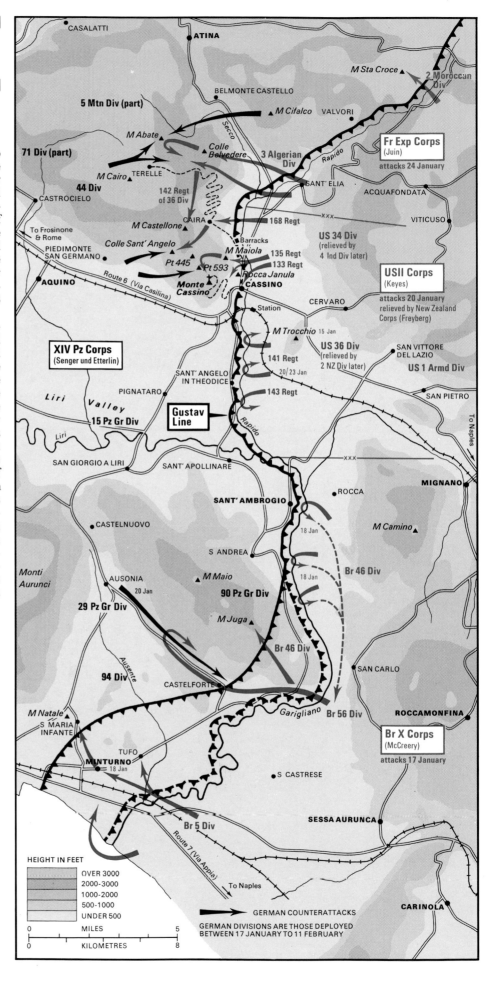

Right: Little remained intact after the abbey at Monte Cassino was finally overrun by the Allies on 18 May.
Below: The second Allied offensive on the Gustav Line was somewhat more successful than its predecessor, pushing the Germans to the Führer-Senger line.

Tenth Army
(Vietinghoff)

To Frosinone & Rome

Liri

ARCE

Route 6 (Via Casilina)

CEPRANO

Sacco

ROCCASECCA

LI Mtn Corps
(Feuerstein)

MELFA

CASTROCIELO

Melfa

S. GIOVANNI INCARICO

PIEDIMONTE SAN GERMANO

AQUINO

CASALATTI

ATINA

BELMONTE CASTELLO

M Cifalco

VALVORI

Secco

M Abate

TERELLE 17 May

Colle Belvedere

M Cairo

CAIRA

Colle Sant' Angelo

5 Pol Div

Pt 445

3 Pol Div

SANT' ELIA

Br X Corps
(McCreery)

Rapido

ACQUAFONDATA

ROCCARAVINDOLA

Pol II Corps
(Anders)

Eighth Army
(Leese)

1 Para Div

Pt 593

M Maiola

Monte Cassino

CASSINO

Station

6 Armd Div

VENAFRO

PASTENA

17 May Germans withdraw

PIUMAROLA
17 May

4 Div

SAN VITTORE DEL LAZIO

Br XIII Corps
(Kirkman)

PONTECORVO
19 May

Blocking Group Bode

S PIETRO

PICO

PIGNATARO
15 May

SANT' ANGELO IN THEODICE

78 Div

Liri

8 Ind Div

Rapido

XXXX

M Cesima

19 May

Cdn I Corps
(Burns)
from reserve

S. OLIVO

M d'Oro

SAN GIORGIO A LIRI
15 May

S. APOLLINARE
13 May

SANT' AMBROGIO

ROCCA

MIGNANO

15 Army Group
(Alexander)

CAMPODIMELE

XIV Pz Corps
(Senger und Etterlin)

ESPERIA
17 May

CASTELNUOVO

S ANDREA
13 May

M Camino

PRESENZARO

M Faggeta

71 Div

M Maio
13 May

M Faito
11/12 May

1 Fr Mot Div

Monti Aurunci

AUSONIA
14 May

San Carlo

MARZANO APPIO

M Petrella
16 May

Ausente

2 Mor Div

M Grande
19 May

M Revole

Fr Exp Corps
(Juin)

ITRI

MARANOLA

94 Div

CASTELFORTE

4 Mor Mtn Div

SAN CARLO

M Sta Croce

ROCCAMONFINA

S MARIA INFANTE
13 May

TUFO

Garigliano

3 Alg Div

US Fifth Army
(Clark)

FORMIA
17 May

US 88 Div

S CASTRESE

PORTO SALVO

MINTURNO

TEANO

SERAPO

GAETA

US 85 Div

SESSA AURUNCA

Route 7 (Via Appia)

CELLOLE

US II Corps
(Keyes)

PETRULO

CARINOLA

SPARANISE

M Massico

NOCELLETO

HEIGHT IN FEET
OVER 3000
2000-3000
1000-2000
500-1000
UNDER 500

FRONT LINE, 11 MAY, 1944
GUSTAV LINE
FUHRER-SENGER LINE

MILES   0   8
KILOMETERS   0   12

Anzio and the Road to Rome

The Allied landings at Anzio on 22 January 1944 were designed to relieve pressure on Cassino, but the results were just the reverse: only the Allied success at Cassino allowed the US VI Corps to break out of its bungled position on the coast. Fifty thousand troops came ashore under Major General John Lucas, who made the fatal error of establishing a beachhead rather than pressing inland so as to wait for his heavy artillery and tanks. The Germans, under Mackensen, seized this welcome opportunity to pin down VI Corps at Anzio and mass forces for a major counterattack on 16 February. Not until the 19th was this halted, to be followed by a state of siege that would last until late May. Lucas was soon replaced by Major General Lucius Truscott, but it was too late to retrieve the situation.

When the Allies finally broke the Gustav Line at Cassino, Clark's Fifth Army could resume its advance northward. Instead of swinging east in an effort to trap the German Tenth Army, Clark opted for capturing Rome – an important moral victory, though hardly necessary strategically. The Germans were able to delay his troops at Velletri and Valmontone long enough to ensure the escape of virtually all their forces in the area. The Allies finally entered Rome on 4 June 1944, just two days before the invasion of France.

Right: The intention of the Anzio operation was to cut German communications by landing behind their front line.
Below: The Allies on the road to Rome.

Above left: Mount Vesuvius' symbolic eruption failed to deter B-25 bombers of the US 12th Air Force en route to Cassino.
Left: A second pall of smoke hangs over the city and monastery as the bombs burst.

ALLIED FRONT
24 JANUARY
1 FEBRUARY
19 FEBRUARY
(STABILIZED)

GERMAN COUNTERATTACKS
3/4 FEBRUARY
7/9
16/19

ROME

FRASCATI

Route 7

FRATTOCHIE

Route 6

VALMONTONE

German positions are
those at 21 January,
other divisions deployed
in area during containment
of beachhead

ALBANO

Alban
Hills

ARTENA

Fourteenth Army
(Mackensen)

LANUVIO   VELLETRI

CORI

CAMPOLEONE

29/30 Jan

Station

Bn 29 Pz
Gr Div

CISTERNA

Buonriposo Ridge
Moletta

CARROCETO

Aprilia Factory

ISOLA
BELLA

1 Feb

PADIGLIONE

The Flyover

Disused railway bed

Regts of
Hermann
Göring Pz Div

Padiglione
Wood

CONCA

BORGO
PIAVE

Commandos

NETTUNO

LATINA

ANZIO

2 US
para bns

Mussolini
Canal

'SHINGLE'
22 January 1944
US VI Corps (Lucas,
Truscott later)

US 3 Div
(Truscott)

Remainder Br 1 Div as floating reserve.
US 1 Armd Div and 45 Div as follow-up reserve

MILES   10
0
KILOMETERS   16

Part of Br 1 Div (Penney)

The End in Italy

After Rome fell, the Allies forced the Germans back to their last defense – the Gothic Line. The Germans were now being reinforced from the Balkans and Germany, while Allied troops, aircraft and landing craft had been drawn off to France. British Eighth Army reached the Gothic Line on 30 August 1944 and attacked with considerable success, but the Germans held commanding positions on the Gemmano and Coriano Ridges that slowed the advance to Rimini until late September.

US Fifth Army had also broken through, but the approach of winter found Clark's exhausted forces short of their objective of Bologna. The Allied advance did not resume until April 1945, by which time Clark had become commander of 15 Army Group. Reinforcements and new equipment had reached him during the winter, and he planned a two-pronged offensive against Ferrara (Eighth Army) and Bologna (Fifth Army).

The German Tenth Army, now under General Herr, was surprised by the British attack across Lake Comocchio, which had been covered by a major artillery bombardment beginning on 9 April. The British moved into the Argenta Gap and Fifth Army, now led by Major General Lucius Truscott, broke through Lemelsen's German Fourteenth Army into the Po Valley (20 April). General von Vietinghoff, who had replaced Kesselring as overall commander in Italy, was forced back to the left bank of the Po, leaving behind all his heavy weapons and armor. The Fascist Ligurian Army had disappeared without a trace, and Axis forces in Italy were out of the fight when Bologna fell on 21 April. Vietinghoff signed the surrender of German forces in Italy on 29 April 1945.

Opposite top left: The unsuccessful Anzio landing on 22 January 1944 which left both sides in a siege position.
Above left: An Axis ammunition train receives a direct hit, March 1944.
Left: Wehrmacht soldiers are marched into captivity north of Anzio.
Top right: Breaking the Gothic Line, the final German defense in Italy.
Above right: The Allies advance into Northern Italy.
Right: US 105mm howitzers fire across the Arno, August 1944.

Ebb Tide in the Pacific

Battle of the Coral Sea

After the Doolittle bombing raid on Tokyo (18 April 1942), Japanese strategists sought ways to extend their defense perimeter in Greater East Asia. One of their options was to strike from Rabaul against Port Moresby, New Guinea; extend their hold on the Solomon Islands; and isolate Australia from the United States. This task was assigned to a five-part force designated MO, under command of Admiral Shigeyoshi Inouye. It comprised a Port Moresby Invasion Group of eleven transports and attendant destroyers; a smaller Tulagi Invasion Group charged with setting up a seaplane base on Tulagi in the southern Solomons;

a Covering Group under Rear Admiral Goto that included the carrier *Shoho*; a smaller support group; and Vice Admiral Takagi's Carrier Striking Force, including *Shokaku* and *Zuikaku*. The operation's complexity suggests that no serious opposition was expected from the Allies, but Admiral Nimitz, Commander in Chief of the Pacific Fleet, moved quickly to counter it. A hastily improvised Task Force of three components, including the carriers *Yorktown* and *Lexington*, prepared to rendezvous in the Coral Sea on 4 May. The Japanese attack came one day earlier.

Tulagi was occupied without opposition, after which the opponents lost several days seeking one another in vain. Then Vice-Admiral Frank Fletcher dispatched British Rear-Admiral John Crace and his Task Force 44 to attack the Port Moresby Invasion Group (7 May). The Japanese mistook this group for the main Allied force and bombed it continuously until Crace made his escape by skillful maneuvering at the end of the day – not

without inflicting some damage in return. Another Japanese error led to an attack on the tanker *Neosho* and the destroyer *Sims* at the same time that the main Allied force, still undetected, converged on Goto's Covering Group and sank *Shoho*.

The Japanese had already ordered the invasion transports to turn back, but now that Fletcher's position was known an air strike was launched against his group on the night of 7-8 May. Twenty-seven Japanese planes took off, of which only six returned. Then *Shokaku* was attacked and disabled; a reciprocal Japanese strike fatally damaged *Lexington* and put *Yorktown* out of action. At no time in the battle did opposing surface ships sight one another – a circumstance new to naval warfare, but soon to become familiar in the Pacific Theater.

Tactically, the Battle of the Coral Sea was a draw: the Japanese lost more planes, the US more ships. Strategically – and morally – it was a major US victory that came when one was needed most.

Battle of Midway

Previous page: The final dive of a stricken Japanese bomber west of the Marianas Islands, June 1944.
Opposite below: Coral Sea was the first naval battle fought without surface vessels sighting each other.

Below: The complex Japanese plan of attack at Midway involved no less than eight task forces.
Bottom: The battle took place north of Midway and ended in decisive defeat for the Japanese.

Midway was the turning point in the Pacific War and a watershed in modern history. Having failed to gain their objectives in the Coral Sea operations of early May 1942, the Japanese were determined to capture Midway as a base within striking distance of Hawaii. The destruction of the Pacific Fleet before US industry could build it up again was recognized as a matter of supreme urgency, besides which the occupation of Midway would eliminate the bombing threat to the home islands. The operation was scheduled for 4 June 1942.

Fleet Admiral Isoroku Yamamoto, architect of the Pearl Harbor attack, formed a complex plan involving eight separate task forces, one of which was to make a diversionary attack on the Aleutian Islands. Almost all of the Japanese surface fleet would be involved – 162 warships and auxiliaries, including four fleet carriers and three light carriers commanded by Admiral Nagumo.

Information – and the lack of it – played a crucial role in the battle's outcome. Yamamoto believed that the carrier *Yorktown* had been destroyed in the Coral Sea along with *Lexington*. In fact, the damaged ship had been refitted for battle at Pearl Harbor in the incredibly short time of 48 hours. Nor did the Japanese realize that the Americans had broken their fleet code: Nimitz was fully aware of their plans. Although he had only 76 ships, three of them were fleet carriers – *Yorktown, Enterprise* and *Hornet*, with a total of 250 planes – whose presence was wholly unsuspected by the Japanese. As a result, Nagumo sent out few reconnaissance flights, which could have warned him of their presence.

Before dawn on 4 June, the Japanese dispatched 108 bombers to Midway, reserving 93 on deck armed for naval contingencies only with armor-piercing bombs and torpedoes. Many US planes were destroyed on the ground in the first attack, but those that survived took off to intercept the incoming bombers. They were largely destroyed by enemy Zeros, but they made a second strike imperative and thereby gave their carriers the chance to attack Nagumo's fleet while it was rearming with high-explosive and fragmentation bombs. When a Japanese reconnaissance plane finally reported detection of enemy carriers, Nagumo's planes were unready to mount a defense.

The first few US carrier strikes inflicted little damage, but the decisive blow caught all the newly armed Japanese planes on their flight decks waiting to take off. Five minutes later, three of the four Japanese carriers were sinking. *Hiryu* escaped immediate destruction and disabled *Yorktown*, but damage inflicted on her by *Enterprise* was so severe that she had to be scuttled the following day. It was the end of Japanese naval supremacy in the Pacific.

JAPANESE FORCES SAIL BETWEEN 25-28 MAY (DATES ARE THOSE AT MIDWAY)

Guadalcanal and the Solomon Islands

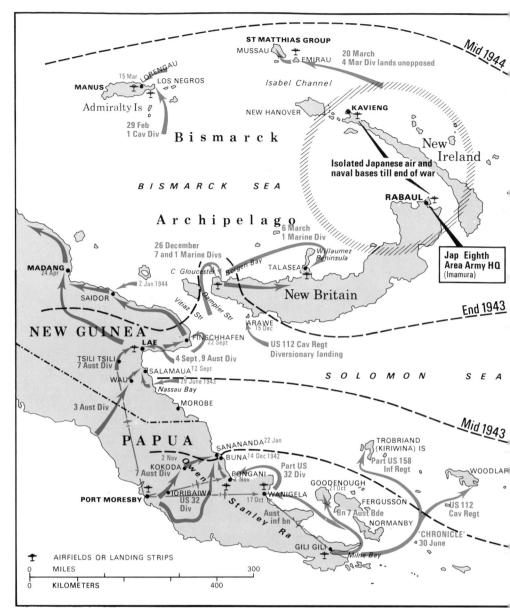

Prior to 1942, few Americans had ever heard of those far-flung islands whose names would become so familiar during the war years – names like Okinawa, Iwo Jima and Guadalcanal. Japanese forces waged a six-month battle for this island in the southern Solomons with US Marines who landed there on 7-8 August 1942. Their objective was a Japanese airbase still under construction to offset the loss of carrier air cover at Midway.

Admiral Fletcher, who had distinguished himself at Midway, was in overall command of operations in the southern Solomons. Rear Admiral R Kelly Turner led an amphibious task force responsible for landing the 19,000-man 1st Marine Division and its equipment. The Marines reached the airbase – renamed Henderson Field – soon after landing and found it deserted, but they came under heavy attack from the Japanese Navy, which dominated surrounding waters by night and soon sent reinforcements ashore to retake the island. The Marines strengthened the airfield's perimeter and used it to gain control of the sea lanes by day.

Two costly but inconclusive carrier battles were fought, one in August (Battle of the Eastern Solomons), the other in October (Battle of Santa Cruz), as the Japanese landed additional troops and supplies on Guadalcanal. On land, there were three major attacks on the Marine

Operation 'CARTWHEEL'

NEW GUINEA

PAPUA

KAVIENG

RABAUL

LAE

Jap Eighteenth Army (Adachi)

PORT MORESBY

Milne Bay

SOLOMON ISLANDS
Jap Seventeenth Army (Hyakutake)

Command boundary

GUADALCANAL

South-west Pacific Area (MacArthur)

South Pacific Area (Halsey)

Final `Elkton Plan´ (26 April 1943)

AUSTRALIA

GREEN IS

15 February
3 NZ Div

BUKA

Bonis

Tenekau

Bougainville

Kieta

Impress Augusta Bay

Kara   Kahili

BIUN

SHORTLAND IS

ERRYBLOSSOM'
vember
arine Div

'GOODTIME'
27 October
8 NZ Bde Group

FAURO

TREASURY IS

VELLA LAVELLA

'BLISSFUL' (diversion for 'Cherryblossom')
28 October
2 Mar Para Bn
(withdraws 3 Nov)
VOZA

SAGIGAI

Choiseul

The Slot

KOLOMBANGARA

15 Aug

MUNDA

13 Aug

RENDOVA

'TOENAILS'
30 June
US 43 Inf Div

4 July

(New Georgia Sound)

New Georgia

VANGUNI

PAVUVU

RUSSELL IS
BANIKA

'CLEANSLATE'
21 February 1943
US assault bns

PACIFIC OCEAN

SOLOMON ISLANDS

Santa Isabel

FLORIDA IS

Malaita

Henderson Field

End 1942

Guadalcanal
7 Aug 1942/7 Feb 1943

San Cristobal

garrison, all of which were thrown back at considerable cost to the Japanese. Despite reinforcement, the Marines were exhausted by December, but the XIV Army Corps relieved them and the Japanese had to withdraw their own depleted forces.

Guadalcanal provided a jumping-off place for successive conquests in the Solomons, culminating with Bougainville in October 1943. The campaign was characterized by surprise landings, followed by hasty construction or repair of airstrips for local defense and as bases for the next attack. Even strongly garrisoned islands like Bougainville, which had 60,000 widely scattered defenders, were seized and isolated, while Japanese strongpoints at Rabaul and Kavieng were bypassed. The Solomons Campaign wound down in mid 1944, after successful Allied landings on New Britain and the Admiralty and St Matthias groups.

Left and inset: Occupying the Solomons was a lengthy process that took the Allies over a year to complete.
Opposite below: An attack by US aircraft at the beginning of the battle for Guadalcanal.
Below: US Marines landing on the island head immediately for cover.

MILES 10
KILOMETERS 20

Florida I

TULAGI
GAVUTU

0740/1200,
2 Marine Regt plus 1 Para Bn
Strong resistance overcome

Savo I

7 August 1942
US 1 Marine Div
(Vandegrift)

I R O N B O T T O M   S O U N D

1/7 Feb 1943,
Japanese forces
withdraw

C
Esperance

TENARO

October,
Japanese reserves
land

Night 7/8 Sept
Marine raiders
attack Jap base

17 Jan 1943,
Jap Seventeenth Army
begins withdrawal from
the Matanikau

Tassafaronga
Pt

PM, 8 Aug
Henderson Field
taken

0909,
5 Marine Regt lands
unopposed
1 Marine Regt follows

Koli Pt

Aug
Sept

TAIVU

Lunga Pt
KUKUM

TENARO

23/26 Oct,
Maruyama's attacks
repulsed

Matanikau

Mt Austen

Bloody Ridge

Night 20/21 Aug,
Ichiki's detachment
destroyed

Lunga

Tenaru

12/14 Sept,
Kawaguchi suffers
heavy losses at
Bloody Ridge

G u a d a l c a n a l

© Richard Natkiel, 1982

AMERICAN ATTACKS
JAPANESE COUNTERATTACKS
AND WITHDRAWALS
US DEFENSE PERIMETER 9 AUGUST
US POSITIONS 23 OCTOBER

EARLY DECEMBER, 1 MARINE DIV RELIEVED BY 25 INF, 2 MARINE AND AMERICAL DIVS (XIV CORPS [PATCH])

*Left: US landings on Guadalcanal and
the resistance encountered.
Below left: Japanese supply ships and
their escorts met US Task Force 67 near
Tassafaronga on 30 November 1942 in
one of the many naval actions off
Guadalcanal. On this occasion, the
Japanese emerged on top.
Bottom left: Marine reinforcements
disembark.
Below: US Navy vessels weave to counter
air attack off the Solomons.
Right: US landings on New Guinea.
Below right: General MacArthur (right)
passes an encouraging word with a
paratrooper at Port Moresby.*

Tanaka's
2nd Dest Flot
and transports

Savo I

0 NAUTICAL MILES 5

Van destroyers

Honolulu

2348
Northampton sunk

Rear destroyers

Suzukaze
Kawakaze
Kagero
Kuroshio
Oyashio
Makinami
Naganami

2306
Takanami

2338
Pensacola torpedoed

2330
New Orleans
torpedoed

'Ironbottom Sound'

2327
Minneapolis
torpedoed

destroyers:
Fletcher
Perkins
Maury
Drayton

Japanese destroyers
turn to engage
US force

0137 Takanami
sunk

2306
Radar
contact

2238

cruisers:
Minneapolis
New Orleans
Pensacola
Honolulu
Northampton

TASSAFARONGA

destroyers:
Lamson
Lardner

Guadalcanal

Task Force 67 (Wright)

New Guinea

The Japanese made a second attempt against Port Moresby in July 1942 – an overland advance from Buna – but it was stopped by Australian formations in September. Allied forces built an airstrip at Milne Bay, then proceeded over the Owen Stanley Range against totally adverse ground and weather conditions to capture Buna and Sanananda at year's end. Australian coast-watchers were instrumental in Allied success by providing early warning of Japanese moves, but all combatants were plagued by tropical disease, grueling terrain and a lack of accurate maps of the area.

After Buna fell, Lae and the Markham Valley were captured with the assistance of Allied air forces (excellent coordination of all the services involved was a feature of this campaign). A series of operations around the Huon Peninsula was followed by major landings at Hollandia and Aitape in April 1944. These cut off some 200,000 Japanese troops and numerous civilian workers centered around Wewak. The final New Guinea landings, at and near the northern tip of the island, secured airfields to be used in support of operations in the Marianas and the Philippines. By July 1944, an entire Japanese Army had been neutralized in New Guinea, and the Solomons Campaign had nullified the threat to Australia and New Zealand.

The Battle of the Philippine Sea

SITUATION 19 JUNE 1944

SITUATION 20 JUNE 1944

After clearing the Marshall Islands, the US trans-Pacific drive converged on the Mariana group, whose conquest would cut off the Japanese homeland from the Philippines and Southeast Asia. When the US assault fell on the main Japanese defenses at Saipan, Tinian and Guam, the Japanese Navy was there to counter it (June–July 1944).

The Japanese First Mobile Fleet, under Vice-Admiral Jisaburo Ozawa, rendezvoused with Vice-Admiral Matome Ugaki's Southern Force on 16 June. Three days later, Ozawa's scouting planes spotted Vice-Admiral Marc Mitscher's US Task Force 58 underway to give battle; strike aircraft were launched immediately. Meanwhile, US submarines had located Ozawa's force and torpedoed his flagship, the carrier *Taiho*. The veteran *Shokaku* was also sunk. An abortive second strike by Ozawa was misdirected, and US fighters intercepted it on its way to Guam. Japanese losses by nightfall of 19 June included 340 irreplaceable veteran pilots and two carriers. US crewmen dubbed the battle 'The Great Marianas Turkey Shoot.'

Ozawa compounded his errors by lingering in the vicinity, with the result that he lost three more ships the following day. The US had lost only 50 planes and suffered slight damage to a single battleship. Ozawa's reputation as an outstanding commander was impaired by this disaster, but his resignation was refused by his superiors and he fought again at the Battle of Leyte Gulf with skill and tenacity. By that time, however, the Japanese defeat was inevitable.

Top left: The opposing fleets rendezvous. Center and above: The course of the battle on 19-20 June.
Top: A Japanese divebomber narrowly misses USS Bunker Hill *of Task Force 58.*
Right: Return of an F6F-3 Hellcat fighter to Lexington *during 'The Great Marianas Turkey Shoot'.*

The Struggle for Leyte and Luzon

General Douglas MacArthur's over-riding desire to liberate the Philippines played a major part in the Allied High Command decision to make landings on Leyte in October 1944. MacArthur's forces joined Nimitz's for this operation, in a rare display of co-operation between these two competitive leaders. Only 20,000 Japanese held the island against 130,000 men of General Walter Krueger's Sixth Army, who landed on 20 October. Japanese reinforcements could not keep pace with this kind of manpower. By Christmas 1944, major engagements were almost over, with Japanese casualties estimated between 50 and 80,000. The Americans had lost only 3600 men.

At sea, four major actions comprised the Battle of Leyte Gulf (21-25 October), in which Japan sought to prevent the Americans from regaining a foothold in the Philippines. Admiral Ozawa's depleted carrier force was to serve largely as a decoy, luring Admiral Halsey's powerful Third Fleet away from the main action. The real fighting was assigned to four task forces of Japanese battleships and cruisers, which were still plentiful. On the US side, Halsey's force was augmented by Admiral Kincaid's Seventh Fleet, backed by carrier formation TF.38.

Left: The land battles for Leyte saw superior US forces emerge triumphant. Above: A Japanese fuel dump on Leyte blazes as a result of naval shelling.

POSITIONS OF US CARRIER TASK GROUPS, 0600, 24 OCTOBER
TIMES ARE THOSE FOR 24 OCTOBER UNLESS OTHERWISE INDICATED

0   NAUTICAL MILES   300

Above right: The sea actions comprising the Battle of Leyte Gulf resulted in a US victory despite the involvement of three separate Japanese forces.

Japanese Force A was turned back by US submarines and carrier aircraft, which then turned north in pursuit of Ozawa's force. Vice-Admiral Nishimura's Force C was almost entirely destroyed in a night battle, and Vice-Admiral Shima's Second Striking Force was turned back. Only Kurita's First Striking Force was still a factor, but it failed to capitalize on its opportunity to wreak havoc on the Seventh Fleet, and withdrew after limited success on 25 October. Meanwhile, many of Ozawa's ships, including the valuable carrier *Zuikaku*, last veteran of Pearl Harbor, had been sunk. Japanese desperation was manifested in the first of the suicidal Kamikaze missions, which struck an Australian cruiser on 21 October.

Lieutenant General Tomoyuki Yamashita, the 'Tiger of Malaya,' had assumed command of Philippine defense just as Leyte was being attacked. When US forces moved to invade Luzon, the

0930 hrs, 9 January 1945
US Sixth Army (Krueger)

I Corps (Swift)
6 Div and 43 Div

XIV Corps (Griswold)
37 Div and 40 Div

17 Jan

29 Jan
XI Corps (Hall)

15 Feb
Regt of XI Corps

21 Feb
Bataan cleared

31 Jan
Majority 11 Abn Div

3 Feb
Remainder drop by
parachute. Light opposition

Command boundary
US Sixth Army

US Eighth Army, 1 Jan 1945

15 December 1944
Western Visayan Task Force
(Dunckel) lands. Light opposition.
Other landings between 21 December
and 22 January

CAMIGUIN

LAOAG
23 June
Part 511 Para Inf Regt
APARRI
GONZAGA

26 June
Contact

VIGAN
19 Apr
TUGUEGARAO
25 June

Cordillera Central

Cagayan

ILAGAN
19 June

BONTOC

Luzon

Sierra Madre

SAN FERNANDO
26 Mar

Lingayen G.
BAUANG
BAGUIO
BAYOMBONG

AGOO
DAMORTIS
ROSARIO
BAMBANG

LINGAYEN
TAYUG

Agno

CARMEN

SAN JOSE
13 Feb

**Jap Fourteenth
Area Army** (Yamashita)

Zambales Mts

TARLAC
21 Jan
CABANATUAN 24 Jan

IBA
BAMBAN
GAPAN

Clark Field
PORAC
Del Carmen Field
SAN FERNANDO

SAN ANTONIO
DANILUPIHAN
CALUMPIT
OLONGAPO
5 Feb

**Bataan
Peninsula**
Manila
Bay
MANILA

4 Feb/3 March
Battle for Manila

CAVITE
Nielson & Nichols Fields

CORREGIDOR
28 Feb

Laguna de Bay
Lamon Bay

NASUGBU
MAUBAN
10 Apr

Tagaytay Ridge
ATIMONAN
DAET

TIAONG
LUCENA
SIAIN
CALAUAG
14 Apr

Balayan Bay
BATANGAS

LUBANG IS
xxxx

CALAPAN
24 Jan

BOAC

Bicol Peninsula
NAGA

CATANDUANES

2 May
Contact

1 April
158 Regt CT

xxxx
LEGASPI

Mindoro
BURIAS
IROSIN

Sibuyan
Sea

San Bernardino Str

SAN JOSE

Jap defense sectors

Shobo Group
(Yamashita)
152,000 men

Kembu Group
(Tsukada)
30,000 men

Shimbu Group
(Yokoyama)
80,000 men

Luzon
6 Jan

MANILA

Samar

2 Jan
Leyte

US Seventh Fleet
(Oldendorf)
carrying US Sixth Army
200,000 men

Mindanao

OCCUPIED BY US
FORCES, 1 JAN 1945

YAMASHITA'S HEADQUARTERS
HELD BY JAPANESE REMNANTS
UP TO END OF WAR

0   MILES   100
0   KILOMETERS   150

Above and inset: The capture of Luzon.
Right: The US make landfall on Leyte.

principal island, in January 1945, his
troops were ill prepared and poorly
armed, and most of his air support had
been destroyed or withdrawn to Formosa.
Doubting that he could hold the beaches,
Yamashita made his stand in the inland
mountain areas with the object of tying
up numerous American forces for as long
as possible. In the event, he did not surrender until the war's end, when he still
had 50,000 fighting men. By that time,
most of Luzon and the other islands had
been recaptured in fighting that reached
its crescendo at Manila in February-
March 1945.

Iwo Jima

The rocky island of Iwo Jima, although far from Japan, was part of the Japanese homeland; it offered the dual advantage to the Allies of demoralizing the enemy and providing a fighter airbase in range of Tokyo – if it could be captured. On the minus side, Iwo Jima was devoid of cover and strongly garrisoned by 22,000 troops under Major General Tadamichi Kuribayashi, who had made the eight-square-mile island impervious to aerial bombardment with a network of pillboxes, caves and tunnels.

The most prolonged and intense bombardment of the Pacific War preceded the US Marine landings of 19 February 1945. The Japanese held their fire just minutes too long, hoping to dupe the invaders into believing they would offer no resistance. By the time their weapons opened up against the beachhead, two Marine divisions and all their equipment had landed, with more to come throughout the day.

The Marines broke out and made straight for Mt Suribachi, the sugar-loaf massif at the island's tip. There they succeeded in raising the US flag after three days of combat so costly that it eclipsed even Tarawa, but the northeast of the island remained unconquered. The maze of underground defenses and lack of room to maneuver made for hand-to-hand combat of savage ferocity. Nearly 7000 US Marines and sailors lost their lives in the fighting that raged until 26 March, and the Japanese died almost to a man. Their exemplar in courage was Kuribayashi, who contacted Tokyo days after their food and water ran out with the message: 'Fighting spirit is running high. We are going to fight bravely to the last moment.'

Right: Iwo Jima, a small island with immense strategic significance.
Below: US Marines advance with flamethrowers toward Mt Suribachi.

Okinawa

The inexorable Allied advance toward the Japanese home islands reached Okinawa, the main island of the Ryukyu group, in March of 1945. Okinawa's capture was necessary to provide harbor and air-base facilities for the invasion of Japan. The island was defended by the Japanese Thirty-second Army – some 130,000 men – under General Mitsuru Ushijima.

Preliminary air operations were aimed at Japanese air bases on Formosa and the islands surrounding densely populated Okinawa. US and British carrier forces suffered losses to waves of Kamikaze attacks, but the Japanese paid a higher price – 90 percent of their planes were shot down before they could sacrifice themselves on the enemy's ships. From 23 March, Okinawa itself was the target of continuous air and artillery strafing.

Allied forces began to land on 1 April, when General Simon Bolivar Buckner's Tenth Army and associated forces gained a beachhead at the southern end of the island. The Japanese had established themselves behind the formidable Shuri Line, which remained almost impervious to attack until early May, when suicidal counterattacks disclosed the locations of many Japanese defensive positions. From this point on, both of the US corps involved gradually pushed forward, as Ushijima's forces retreated into the hill masses of the island's southern tip. Final resistance was overwhelmed by a massive two-pronged attack on 21 June.

Throughout the operation, code-named Iceberg, supporting naval forces were under constant attack by Kamikaze pilots, who accounted for 36 US and British ships and damaged hundreds of others. The Japanese lost a staggering 4000 aircraft in these suicide missions, and even sacrificed the giant battleship *Yamato*, which was dispatched to Okinawa with insufficient fuel for a return trip to do as much damage as possible before she was destroyed. This happened on 7 April, long before the battleship could reach the target area.

On land, known Japanese dead totaled almost 108,000, and for the first time a significant number of prisoners was taken – over 7000. General Buckner was killed, with over 7000 of his men; almost 32,000 were wounded. US Navy casualties were almost 10,000, of whom roughly half were killed and half wounded. Since Okinawa was considered a 'dress rehearsal' for the invasion of Japan, these

figures were sobering to American strategists; General MacArthur estimated that it would take five million men to capture the home islands, of whom perhaps one million would become casualties. Thus Okinawa strengthened the Allied case for ending the war by other means.

Above: The invasion of Okinawa was seen as the dress rehearsal for a similar action against the Japanese home islands.
Above right: Marines await survivors of an explosive attack on a Japanese hideout on Okinawa.
Right: The Japanese battleship Yamato *was sacrificed in a vain attempt to stem the invasion.*

Air Strikes on the Home Islands

The bomber offensive against Japan could not begin until 1944, for lack of a very-long-range (VLR) bomber capable of carrying heavy loads for over 3000 miles. Such a plane was finally acquired from Boeing by the US Army Air Force (the B-29 Superfortress), but it was so newly developed that operational problems plagued its early operations. The B-29's bombing altitude of 30,000 feet created difficulties with high winds and the effect of ice on instruments and engines. Losses were running high for several months after the first raid, from eastern China, in June of 1944. Additionally, Japanese anti-aircraft defenses proved much more effective than had been anticipated.

Modified tactics resulted in operating the planes at much lower altitudes with heavier bomb loads, which paid off in improved performance. New bases were established in the Marianas Islands of the Central Pacific in November, after which up to 20 Bombardment Groups flew regularly over Japanese cities by day and night. They dropped a total of 9365 tons of incendiaries, which gutted 32 square miles of urban areas. Then escort fighters began to arrive from newly captured Iwo Jima (early April) and American losses reached a new low. As more B-29s became available, mortal blows were dealt to Japanese industry. On 6 and 9 August 1945, the war with Japan was ended – and a new era in human history begun – by the atomic bombing of Hiroshima and Nagasaki.

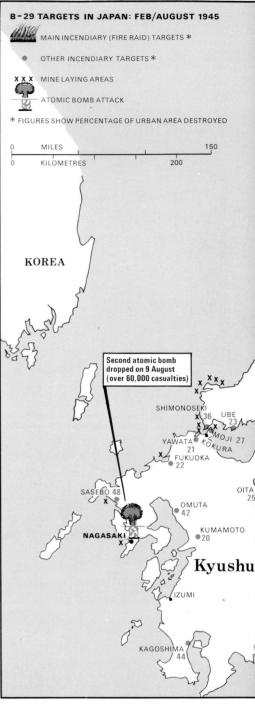

B-29 TARGETS IN JAPAN: FEB/AUGUST 1945

MAIN INCENDIARY (FIRE RAID) TARGETS *

OTHER INCENDIARY TARGETS *

X X X   MINE LAYING AREAS

ATOMIC BOMB ATTACK

* FIGURES SHOW PERCENTAGE OF URBAN AREA DESTROYED

KOREA

Second atomic bomb dropped on 9 August (over 60,000 casualties)

SHIMONOSEKI
UBE 23
36
YAWATA 21 MOJI 27
KOKURA
FUKUOKA 22
SASEBO 48
OITA 25
OMUTA 42
NAGASAKI
KUMAMOTO 20
Kyushu
IZUMI
KAGOSHIMA 44

Left: The now-familiar atomic mushroom cloud rises over Nagasaki.
Above: The Japanese homeland and (inset) the radius of US bomber operations over it.
Right: Doolittle's daring one-off raid in April 1942 from the USS Hornet *had been as much a propaganda exercise as an attack. The firebomb raids of 1945 were on a different scale altogether.*
Far right: Tokyo in ruins.

NIIGATA

NAGAOKA
66

Honshu

First fire raid :
25 February 1945
Great fire raid
night 9/10 March
Raided again
25 May
(200,000 casualties)

HITACHI
65

UTSUNOMIYA
34

MITO
65

MAEBASHI
43

ISEZAKI
17

KUMAGAYA
45

HACHIOJI
80

KOFU
65

TOKYO
51

CHOSHI
34

KAWASAKI 33

CHIBA
43

YOKOHAMA
44

HIRATSUKA
44

SHIMIZU
50

NUMAZU
90

SHIZUOKA
66

HAMAMATSU
70

SEA OF JAPAN

NANAO

FUSHIKI

TOYAMA
99

FUKUI
85

TSURUGA
68

GIFU
74

OGAKI
40

ICHINOMIYA
76

NAGOYA
31

OKAZAKI
68

TOYOHASHI
52

First atomic bomb
dropped on 6 August
(over 92,000 casualties)

Fire raid :
night 16/17 March
(15,000 casualties)

Fire raid :
night 11/12 March
and 19 March
(light casualties)

MIYAZU

MAIZURU

NISHINOMIYA 30

KUWANA 77

YOKKAICHI
60

TSU
57

UJI YAMADA
39

KOBE 56

HIMEJI
63

OKAYAMA
63

AKASHI
57

**OSAKA/
AMAGASAKI** 26

FUKUYAMA
73

HIROSHIMA

TAKAMATSU
78

INLAND SEA

WAKAYAMA
53

KURE
40

IMABARI
76

TOKUSHIMA
74

MATSUYAMA
73

O'SHIMA

KOCHI
48

AKI

Shikoku

Fire raid :
night 14/15 March
(13,000 casualties)

UWAJIMA
52

PACIFIC

OCEAN

USSR

MANCHURIA

JAPANESE TERRITORIES
MARCH 1945

KOREA

JAPAN

TOKYO

PEKING

PACIFIC

OCEAN

CHINA

SHANGHAI

RYUKYU IS.

YAKOSHIMA

OKINAWA

IWO JIMA

Fighter cover by P-51 Mustangs
and P-61 'Black Widows' from
April 1945 and P-47 Thunderbolts
later

FORMOSA

MARIANAS IS

1,600 MILES

**PHILIPPINE
IS**

SAIPAN
TINIAN

GUAM

US 20 Air Force bases
(Le May)
incl 20 and 21 Bomber
Commands (B-29s)
from February 1945

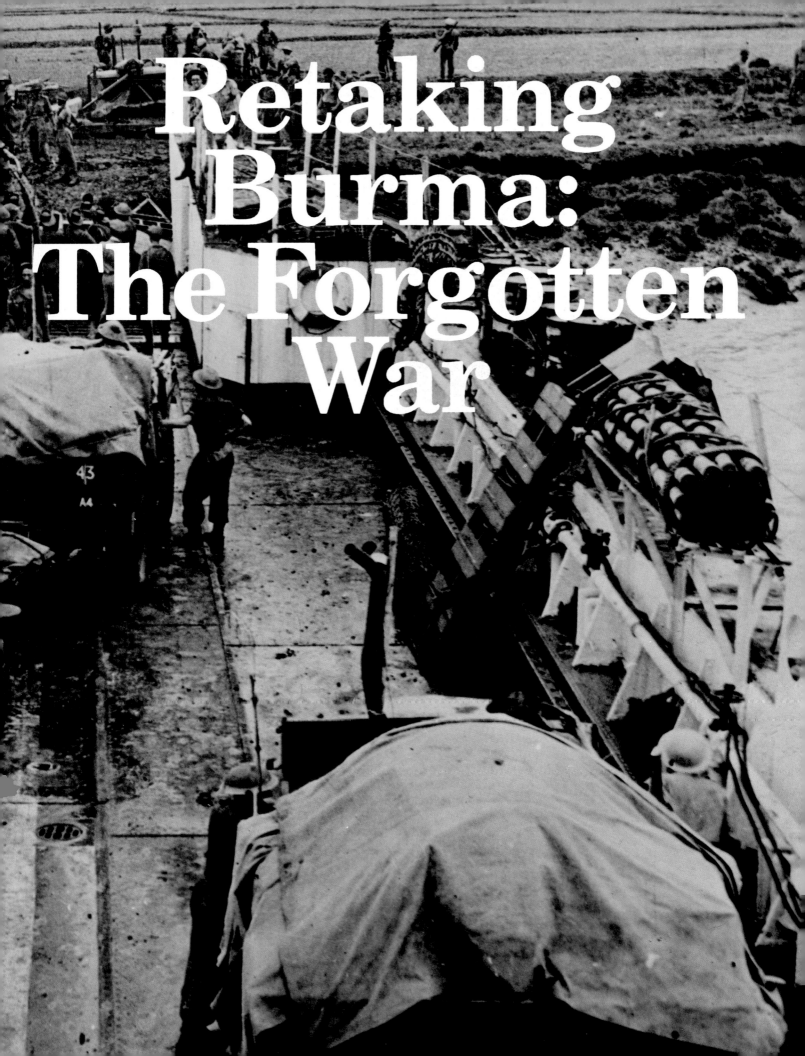

Retaking Burma: The Forgotten War

The Arakan Battles

British and US leaders disagreed on strategy in the Burma Theater after the British had been driven into India in May of 1942. The Americans believed that Burmese operations should focus on reopening land communications with the Chinese Nationalists, who were trying to contain large Japanese forces on their home ground. The British had little faith in Chiang Kai-shek's Nationalist movement and maintained their hope of winning back the imperial territories lost to Japan in the 1942 débâcle.

General Archibald Wavell, commanding Allied forces in India, knew that a large-scale invasion was out of the question for the time, but he sought to employ his men and build up morale via small-scale operations near the Indian border. The first of these centered on the Arakan, where the island post of Akyab provided Japan with a position from which to bomb Chittagong and Calcutta. On 21 September Wavell's 14 Indian Division began to advance cautiously into Burma by way of Cox's Bazar. General Iida, the Japanese commander, countered with a series of delaying tactics that created a stalemate lasting until March 1943 when his counterattack on two fronts forced a retreat.

In December 1943, the British sent Christison's XV Corps on a second expedition against Akyab. Lieutenant General Renya Mutaguchi barred the way through the Mayu Peninsula and sent his Sakurai Column through mountainous jungle that was believed impassable to cut off 5 and 7 Indian Divisions. Lieutenant General William Slim, who had led the 900-mile fighting retreat from Rangoon, airlifted supplies to his isolated troops until they had fought their way through to one another in late February 1944. (Slim's use of air supply would ultimately be the key to British success in Burma.) In March XV Corps finally renewed its advance on Akyab, but was stopped short again by the need to send reinforcements back to India for the defense of Imphal.

Previous pages: A 25-pounder gun is brought ashore in Rangoon.
Above right: The Allied route southwards along fair-weather tracks was hampered by enemy action.
Right: 5 and 7 Indian Divisions reunite after being isolated by a Japanese thrust.
Opposite: Japanese troops used elephants as a means of transporting supplies across Burma's rugged terrain.

The Chindit Operations

Morale had been a problem in Burma even before the Allies took what Stilwell described as 'a hell of a beating.' During the disastrous campaign of 1942, fighting spirit reached a new low. The Japanese were perceived as unbeatable in jungle warfare, and the Allied forces' sick rate reflected the prevailing malaise: thousands succumbed to dysentery, malaria, skin diseases and other complaints. The heterogeneous assortment of troops involved in Burma—Indian, British and Gurkha – comprised an army beset by problems of discipline and discrimination.

Brigadier Orde Wingate arrived in the Far East early in 1943 with guerrilla-warfare experience gained in Palestine and Abyssinia. Backed by Winston Churchill and General Wavell, he created a 'private army' to penetrate behind enemy lines and disrupt Japanese communications and supplies. In so doing, he would also prove that the Japanese could be defeated in the jungle.

The Chindits (so called after *Chinthe*, a mythical beast) crossed the River Chindwin into Burma in February 1943 and spent four months raiding Japanese territory. They cut the Mandalay-Myitkyina Railway in 75 places before the Japanese counterattacked in force and drove them back into India. The press lionized Wingate, and the mystique of Japanese invincibility began to lose its power. Wingate's superiors then authorized a far more ambitious operation – involving six brigades – to complement Stilwell's advance on Myitkyina.

The main Chindit force was airlifted into Burma in February 1944 to establish blocking points against supplies moving up against Stilwell. They encountered immediate difficulties that grew steadily worse until midsummer, when they had to be withdrawn. Wingate himself was killed in a plane crash soon after the abortive operation began.

Japanese Defeat at Kohima and Imphal

Above left: The Chindit operations in Burma in 1943.
Left: Wingate (center) briefs pilots on invasion plans with the assistance of the USAAF's Colonel Cochran (left).
Above: Troop movements around Kohima.

Three Japanese divisions were ordered to prepare for the invasion of India (Operation U-GO) in early March 1944. It was clear that an Allied offensive was being prepared, and the only practical place from which it could be launched was the plain at Manipur, where Imphal and Kohima were located. Lieutenant General Mutaguchi's Fifteenth Army was to spoil the planned offensive and cut the single railway to Assam, north India.

General William Slim, commanding Fourteenth Army, expected a Japanese advance, but its speed was such that he and his men were taken by surprise.

Scoones's XV Corps was cut off at Kohima on 4 April, and the garrison at Imphal a day later. Both forces prepared to hold out with the help of air supply until relief arrived from XXXIII Corps, which was assembling at Dimapur. The quality of Slim's leadership would be reflected in the tenacity of his hard-pressed troops until that help arrived.

Relentless Japanese attacks rolled over the small garrison at Kohima between 7 and 18 April, when British 2 Division's 5 Brigade pushed through the roadblock at Zubza to reinforce the defenders. Then 5 and 4 Brigades undertook a sweeping pincer movement designed to trap the Japanese; this was not achieved until 3 June. Meanwhile, IV Corps was struggling desperately around Imphal, where air supply proved far more difficult than foreseen. Slim reinforced the garrison to some 100,000 men during the siege, which lasted for 88 days. British 2 Division advanced from Kohima to meet IV Corps at Milestone 107, halfway between the two cities, on 22 June. Japanese Fifteenth Army had fought with distinction against increasing odds, but its remnants now had to pull back toward the Chindwin, with British forces in hot pursuit. Mutaguchi had lost some 65,000 men in the heaviest defeat suffered by the Japanese Army in World War II.

Right: The unsuccessful Japanese siege of Imphal that ended in June.
Below: Merrill's Marauders, the US jungle fighters renowned for their expertise in combating the Japanese in unfriendly terrain.

KANGPOKPI
Milestone 107
LEISHAN
UKHRUL

JAPANESE ATTACKS
IV CORPS COUNTERATTACKS
APPROXIMATE PERIMETER : 4 APRIL 1944
ALL-WEATHER ROADS
FAIR-WEATHER ROADS
TRACKS
AIRFIELDS
MARSH

22 June
Contact by 2 Br Div
(from Kohima)
and 5 Ind Div

Milestone 116

Jap 15 Div

SANGSHAK

MILES   15
KILOMETRES   20

KANGLATONGBI
Mapao Ridge
11 Apr
20 Ind Div
(from Shenam
20 May)
LITAN

HEIGHTS IN FEET OVER
OVER 5000
3000–5000
1000–3000

SENGMAI
5 Ind Div
Nungshigum
13 Apr
Toyungbi

HQ
End April
23 Ind Div

IV Corps
(Scoones)

IMPHAL

BURI BAZAR
YAIRIPOK

Night 15/16 April
Japanese party blow up
suspension bridge

OINAM

17 Ind Div
(from reserve 18 Apr)
BISHENPUR
POTSANGBUM
WANGJING

TAIRENPOKPI

NINGTHOUKHONG

9/30 April
Japanese attacks
repulsed

20 Ind Div
Relieved by 23 Ind Div,
mid May

Manipur

SITA

PALEL

TORBUNG

Shenam
Saddle
Scraggy
Crete
E and W
Nippon
Hill

5 April/22 June
Heavy Japanese
attacks repulsed

Jap 33 Div

CHURACHANDPUR

SIBONG

To Tiddim
120 miles

SHUGANU

Jap 33 Div

To Silchar 60 miles

To Tiddim

To Mandalay and Meiktila

Lieutenant General Shihachi Katamura took command of Japanese Fifteenth Army after the disastrous losses at Kohima and Imphal, for which his predecessor was unjustly blamed. During the summer of 1944, he rebuilt his force of 10 divisions and then awaited the expected Allied push into central Burma. This operation, codenamed Extended Capital, began on 19 November and included Stilwell's Northern Combat Area Command, British Fourteenth Army and the XV Corps. On 4 December bridgeheads were secured across the Chindwin, and the British advanced to meet elements of Stilwell's force for the drive across the Irrawaddy into Mandalay. Only General Slim, of all the Allied leaders in Burma, correctly surmised that Katamura would attempt to destroy the Fourteenth Army at the river crossing.

On 3 March 1945, Slim struck at Japanese communication lines to Rangoon located at Meiktila, achieving total surprise. The capture of this vital rail center opened the door to the larger city of Mandalay. Kimura pulled so many troops away from Mandalay to assault Meiktila that he lost both cities to the Allies. Slim raced on to reach Rangoon before the monsoon, but when he arrived the Japanese had already evacuated. Slim's outstanding leadership in the Burma Theater led to his appointment as Commander in Chief of Allied Land Forces in Southeast Asia.

Above right: Operation Extended Capital took the Allies across the Chindwin and on to Mandalay.
Right: Flamethrower and rifle-equipped infantry of the United States Army prepare for action.

FOURTEENTH ARMY BRIDGEHEADS
FOURTEENTH ARMY ATTACKS
21 FEBRUARY/30 MARCH
JAPANESE COUNTERATTACKS
ALL-WEATHER ROADS
AIRSTRIPS

0 — MILES — 40
0 — KILOMETERS — 60

YEU

26 February,
19 Ind Div
(Rees) attacks

THABEIKKYIN

98 Bde

KYAUKMYAUNG

SHWEBO

WETLET

INGU

NYAUNGWUN

*Shan
Hills*

62 and
64 Bdes

62 Bde

BUDALIN

XXXIII Corps
(Stopford)

MONYWA

8 March,
20 Ind Div
(Gracey)
attacks

8 March,
Br 2 Div
(Nicholson)
attacks

Stiletto
Force

MADAYA

64 Bde
98 Bde

KABAING

MAYMYO

To Lashio

MYINMU

NGAZUN

5 and
6 Bdes

MANDALAY
20 Mar

AVA 18 Mar

SIZON

32 and
80 Bdes

IV Corps
(Messervy)

Irrawaddy

Chindwin

MYOTHA

KYAUKSE 30 Mar

**Jap Fifteenth
Army** (Katamura)

100 Bde

21 February 1945,
17 Ind Div, 255 Ind Tk Bde
(Cowan) and 7 Ind Div (Evans)
attack

MYINGYAN 22 Mar

NATOGYI

PYINZI

KUME

PAKOKKU

Sindewa

5 March
village
retaken

KANDAW

28 E Afr Bde
MYITCHE

Yaw

33 Bde

KAMYE

TAUNGTHA

17 Div

THEDAW

WUNDWIN

**Jap Thirty-third
Army** (Honda) at
Kalaw from 14 March

NYAUNGU

48 Bde

PYINBIN

OYIN

WELAUNG

MAHLAING
26 Feb

LETSE

63 Bde

SEIKTEIN

7 Div

THABUKTONG

9 and 99 Bde
(5 Ind Div)
flown in

48 Bde

255 Ind
Tank Bde

5/29 March
Jap counterattack
isolates Meiktila

114 Bde

Mt Popa

63 Bde

CHAUK

KYAUKPADANG

MEIKTILA
3 Mar

THAZI

**Jap Twenty-eighth
Army** (Sakurai)

Burma Area Army
(Kimura)

To Rangoon

*Left: Control of Meiktila was to prove of
crucial importance in the battle for
Mandalay.*
*Below: US troops pause on a Burmese
jungle trail.*
*Below right: General Claire Chennault,
whose 'Flying Tigers' struck at Japanese
ground troops in China and Formosa.*
*Far right: China's struggle to repel the
Japanese invaders.*

China – An Erratic Ally

Japan's war on China predated World War II by several years, and by 1939 the aggressive island empire had seized control of China's richest areas. The 'sleeping giant' was especially vulnerable on account of the internal strife between the Nationalists (or Kuomintang) led by Generalissimo Chiang Kai-shek and Mao Tse-tung's Communists.

US General George C Marshall warned the Allies that Nationalist China must be propped up; otherwise, the Japanese Government could flee to China when the home islands were invaded – as was then planned – 'and continue the war on a great and rich land mass.' Throughout the war, the US shipped enormous quantities of supplies to China, first by the Burma Road, and after 1942 by air over the Himalayas – a dangerous route known as 'the Hump.' Chiang's position was strengthened by the creation of the US 14th Air Force, impressively commanded by Brigadier General Claire Chennault, which inflicted heavy damage on Japanese troops both in China and Formosa. General Joseph 'Vinegar Joe' Stilwell was sent in to help retrain the Chinese Army. However, many of the supplies destined for use against the Japanese were diverted into Chiang's war on the Communists; corruption flourished in his Nationalist Party.

US air strikes by Chennault's 'Flying Tigers' provoked a Japanese offensive against the airfields at Liuchow, Kweilin, Lingling and other sites in the spring of 1944. Chinese resistance did not hold up, as was often the case, and the loss of

these bases hampered Allied operations until December. Meanwhile, a truce was patched up between the Communists and Nationalists, allowing greater activity against the Japanese, who renewed their offensive in 1945.

In the war's final year, Japanese General Okamura overextended the deployment of his China Expeditionary Army, and the Chinese were able to cut off the corridor to Indochina. They held this position for the duration, after which the Nationalists and the Communists promptly resumed their civil war.

Russia Finds Its Strength

The German Drive to the Volga

Germany's critical oil shortage was decisive in Hitler's first 1942 campaign plan for the Eastern Front. In April he instructed that the main effort was to be in southern Russia, where German forces must defeat the Red Army on the River Don and advance to the coveted Caucasian oil fields. For this campaign, Bock's Army Group South was reorganized into Army Groups A and B, A to undertake the Caucasus offensive and B to establish a protective front along the Don and go on to Stalingrad. The neutralization of 'Stalin's City' soon gained a compelling hold on Hitler's mind, despite his staff's objections to dividing the German effort before the Red Army had been shattered. Stalingrad was a major rail and river center, whose tank and armaments factories offered additional inducements to attack it.

The obsession with Stalingrad was a disastrous mistake on Hitler's part, compounded by his seizure of control from his dissenting officers. Army Group A made a rapid advance from 28 June to 29 July, capturing Novorossiysk and threatening the Russian Trans-Caucasus Front. But the diversion of 300,000 German troops to the Stalingrad offensive prevented them from achieving their original objective – the Batumi-Baku Line. They were left to hold a 500-mile Caucasian front against strong Russian opposition – leaderless, except for the erratic and contradictory orders of Hitler himself.

The Russians had made good their 1941 manpower losses from the subject peoples of Asia, and they threw the T-34 tank into the field at this point to complete the German fiasco in the Caucasus. The vital oil fields were lost to Germany. Army Group B raced toward Stalingrad to attempt what had now become the only possible success of the campaign. The city could not be encircled without crossing the Volga, which General Weichs lacked the resources to attempt, so a frontal assault was launched on 31 August.

Previous pages: Red Army sappers clear German barbed wire defenses.
Above right: The original German battle plan, with oilfields the main objective.
Above far right: Splitting the forces to strengthen the attack on Stalingrad proved a major error.
Right: The German advance southeastwards with armor and artillery.
Opposite: Commander Chuikov of the Russian 62nd Army at the Volga.

Stalin's City Holds Out

Below: The German forces attack.
Below left: Stalingrad's position on the banks of the Volga enhanced its defensive capabilities.
Bottom: Manstein's forces are repulsed.

The slow pace of the German summer offensive of 1942 allowed Stalingrad's defenders to strengthen their position considerably. The city was home to half a million Russians, who were united in their determination to repel the German assault. Most of the Soviet soldiers were assigned to the defense perimeter, the city itself being entrusted largely to armed civilians, whose high morale promised fierce resistance.

The Volga wound through many channels around the city, posing serious obstacles to any attempt at bridging it. The Germans made no effort to establish a bridgehead north of the city so as to block river traffic and reinforcement.

This was only one of many mistakes, the worst of which was the decision to carry the city by direct attack. The resultant battle would become the Verdun of World War II.

By the end of August, the Russian defenders had been squeezed into a small perimeter, and twelve days later the Germans were in the city, striving to fight their way to the western bank of the Volga. Soviet civilians and soldiers struggled side by side in a constant barrage of bombs and artillery fire, falling back a foot at a time. House-to-house fighting raged until 13 October, when the exhausted German infantry reached the river in the south city. But the northern industrial sector remained unconquered. Hitler ordered intensified bombardments that served only to make the infantry's task more difficult. Stalingrad's defenders continued to fight regardless.

By 18 November, when the winter freeze was imminent, Hitler's armies around Stalingrad were undersupplied, overextended and vulnerable to the Russian counterattack that was forming. Before the Germans were forced to surrender (February 1943), they had lost 100,000 of the 200,000 men involved. Five hundred Luftwaffe transport planes had been destroyed in impotent efforts to supply them, and six months' worth of German war production had been thrown away. Wehrmacht morale was shattered, not only by the great defeat itself, but by the wanton intrusions into military planning that had wrecked the campaign from Berlin.

The Battle of Kursk

The success of the 1942 Russian winter offensive left a large salient around Kursk that tempted the German High Command into mounting a major attack. The fact that US and British aid was now flowing freely into Russia lent urgency to this plan of attack, as Germany's resources were steadily draining away.

The armored pincer movement against the Kursk Salient – codenamed Operation Citadel – was scheduled for July of 1943. Early intelligence of it enabled the Russians to prepare by moving in two armies and setting up eight concentric circles of defense. When the Germans launched their attack on 5 July, it was in the belief that they would achieve surprise. On the contrary, Russian defenses at Kursk were the most formidable they had ever assaulted. The Soviet T-34 tank was superior to anything the German Panzer groups could field, and air command was seized at the outset by multitudes of Russian planes. They were not equal to the Luftwaffe in technology, but they were far superior in numbers.

In the north, German Ninth Army advanced only six miles in the first few days, at a cost of 25,000 killed and 400 tanks and aircraft. In the south, Manstein's Fourth Panzer Army drove through the Russian Sixth Army – again at high cost – only to face fresh Soviet

Opposite far left: The German offensive against Kursk, launched on 5 July.
Left: By 20 July German forces were in full retreat.
Right: The heavily armored KV-1 tanks gave the Germans many problems.
Below: Soviet T-34s take part in the biggest tank battle of the war near Prokhorovka in the south.

tank units from the Russian Steppe Front reserve. The largest tank armies in history clashed near Prokhorovka on 12 July and fought for seven days. Initial German success was followed by increasing Soviet ascendancy, and by 20 July all German forces were in full retreat. Two million men had been involved, with 6000 tanks and 4000 aircraft. Many of the surviving German tanks were dispatched immediately to Italy to counter the Allied offensive that had begun with landings in Sicily. The Russians maintained their momentum in successful advances south of Moscow.

The Dniepr and Smolensk

By fall of 1943, the Soviets had pushed their front line far to the west against diminishing German forces that managed to stay intact and resist, although they could not prevail. In mid September the Russians threatened Smolensk in the north and Kiev in the center. They crossed the Donets in the south and by 30 September had captured Smolensk and established themselves along most of the Dniepr.

German Army Group A, virtually abandoned at its bridgehead in the Caucasus since the previous summer, was pulled out to operate on the right of Manstein's Army Group South, its parent formation. Manstein had recaptured Kharkov in February – against numerical odds of seven to one – but his losses had been staggering. When the Russians took Kiev (6 November) and penetrated his sector, he called for evacuation of the Seventeenth Army from the Crimea. Hitler's characteristic 'No retreat' order was Manstein's reward for months of superhuman effort. Seventeenth Army was cut off in the Crimean Peninsula, just as he had foreseen, and by year's end the Russians had effectively regained all the territory lost in 1942 and more.

Left: The scope of Soviet reoccupation at their western border.
Above: The eventual German withdrawal was made all the more inevitable by the removal of armor and personnel to the Italian Front.
Opposite: A German NCO leads his infantry section at the front line.

The Relief of Leningrad

Leningrad had been isolated from the rest of Russia since 1941 by the German-held corridor between Tosno and Lake Ladoga. For 900 days its people were deprived of food, fuel and arms; by the end of the siege, they were dying of hunger and cold at the rate of 20,000 a day. Throughout this ordeal, Leningrad's citizens continued to produce goods in their factories, even at greatly reduced levels, and to provide for civil defense. A trickle of supplies began to arrive in January 1943, thanks to a concerted effort by the Leningrad and Volkhov Fronts to secure a supply line south of Lake Ladoga. It was little enough, but it prevented total starvation. Not until a year later did real relief reach Leningrad.

In mid-January 1944, three Russian Fronts – Leningrad, Volkhov and 2 Baltic – launched attacks against German Army Group North, commanded first by Küchler and after 29 January by Field Marshal Walther Model. By that time the Russians had cleared the Moscow-Leningrad Railway and recaptured Novgorod. Now threatened by encirclement, Model withdrew Army Group North east of Lake Chudskoye and subsequently stopped the Soviet advance into the Baltic States. Beleaguered Leningrad was restored to the Soviet Union.

Above: Supplies reached Leningrad in limited quantities through the so-called 'Corridor of Death'.
Above right: The earlier division of the Leningrad and Volkhov Fronts.
Right: Final relief of the siege was achieved early in 1944.
Opposite: Defenders dig in at Leningrad's perimeter.

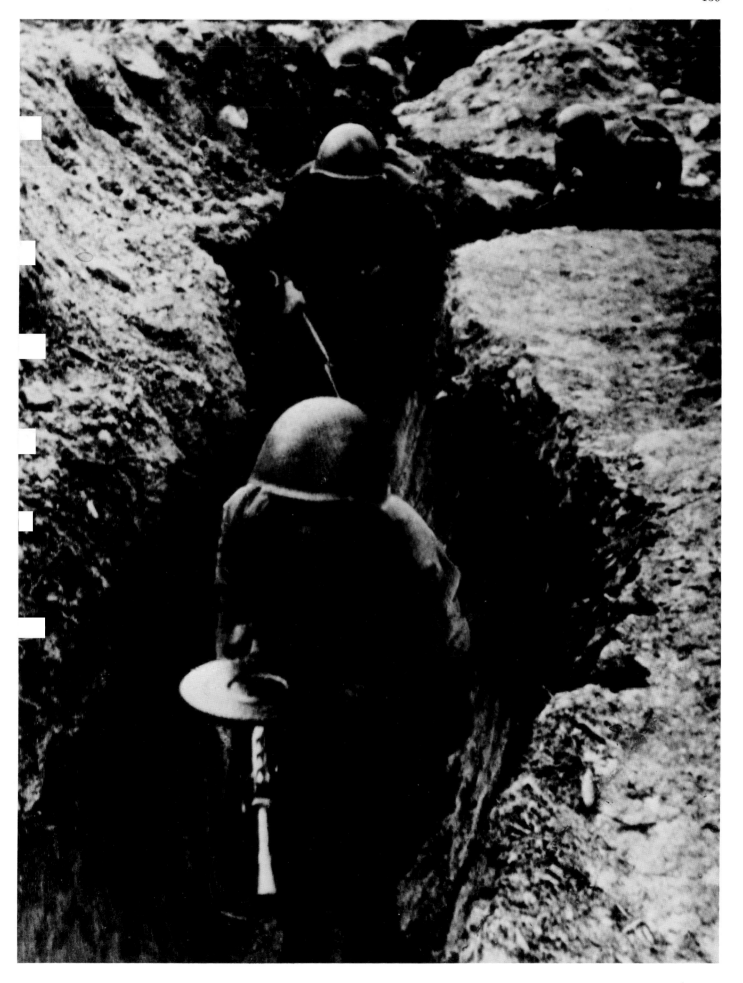

Regaining the Ukraine

During the drive to relieve Leningrad, Russian forces in the south were equally active. The 1 and 2 Ukrainian Fronts launched attacks on all German forces in the Ukraine between 24 December 1943 and 5 January 1944. German First Panzer Army was trapped, and both Manstein's Army Group North Ukraine and Kleist's Army Group A were hard pressed. Manstein tried to counterattack under blizzard conditions, but could do little to slow the Russian advance to the Rivers Bug and Dniestr.

An improvised airlift kept First Panzer Army supplied until it could fight its way out behind Russian lines. German tenacity in south Russia at this time was almost unbelievable, but it was a losing fight. Kleist had to fall back to Odessa, leaving elements of Sixth and Eighth Armies surrounded. On 10 April he was forced out of Odessa, and the Russian front was extended almost as far as Brest Litovsk.

The last rail link between the Germans in Poland and those in southern Russia had been severed in March with the cap-

ture of Chernovtsy by First Ukraine Front. The abandoned German Seventeenth Army was driven from the Crimea, and Sevastopol fell to the Soviets on 12 May.

Hitler was enraged by the losses in the Ukraine, whose rich mineral resources were desperately needed by the Reich. Instead of rewarding Manstein's heroic role there, he relieved him of his command and put the trouble-shooting Model in his place. Kleist was ousted in favor of the ambitious Field Marshal Friedrich Schörner.

Left: A column of Germans captured near the pocket of resistance at Korsun-Shevchenkosky.
Above: Soviet advances on a grand scale.
Right: German soldiers advance through the maize fields of the Ukraine.

From Warsaw to the Oder

Below: The frontiers of German
occupation are pushed back.
Bottom: Marshal Ivan Konev,
Commander of 1 Ukrainian Front, 1944.
Right: Russian forces halt at the Oder
prior to the final push to Berlin.
Below right: Troops of 4 Ukrainian Front
plod over the Polish Carpathians in the
winter of 1944-45.

Early summer of 1944 found widely scattered German forces trying to hold a 1400-mile Eastern Front with very few reserves. On 23 June the Soviets struck along the central sector with three fronts under overall command of Marshal Georgi Zhukov, now deputy supreme commander in the USSR. With a density of almost 400 guns per mile, these troops assaulted General Busch's Army Group Centre just as partisan activity in its rear disrupted communications entirely. There was no contest in the air, as many Luftwaffe units had already been taken west. Busch lost half a million men, killed or captured, from his 33 divisions and was replaced by Model immediately. By the end of August, Zhukov's offensive was at the gates of Warsaw – in the the north, at Riga. Model barely succeeded in preventing the Russians from entering Warsaw; their own pause to resupply outside the city was providential for him. Farther south, Soviet troops had crossed the Vistula for a combined advance of 450 miles in two months. Operations had to be suspended until supply lines could catch up.

By January 1945 the Russians were poised to invade Germany for the first time since 1914. Rokossovsky's 2 Belorussian Front of nine armies assaulted the German Second Army north of Warsaw, while the Russian Forty-seventh Army encircled the city, which fell on 17 January. Army Group Centre was driven back into a few pockets along the Bay of Danzig, from which the German Navy extricated some half a million men in March and April. On 9 May the last German beachheads surrendered.

As Rokossovsky attacked north of the Vistula, the 1 Belorussian and 1 Ukrainian Fronts advanced at top speed on a wide front from Warsaw to Jasto. They had reached the Oder by 31 January, bypassing pockets of German resistance. Russian armies of over 1,500,000 men confronted German forces of 596,000, with still greater inequalities in armaments and aircraft. By 24 February Pomerania and Silesia had fallen, giving Soviet forces a solid front along the Oder less than 40 miles from Berlin. Only one sizeable German force would be left in Europe after the fall of Berlin: Schörner's Army Group Centre, which had moved into Czechoslovakia. The Russian 'liberation' of that country would be a microcosm of what transpired in Eastern Europe after the German defeat.

The Drive into Czechoslovakia

Desperate Nazi plans focused on the formation of a 'national redoubt' on the German/Czechoslovak border after the fall of Berlin. These plans were based on Schörner's armies of almost a million men, which held the Reich's last important industrial area. In reality, however, their situation was hopeless, surrounded as they were by the Russians on three sides and with Patton's US Third Army approaching from the west.

By 6 March 1945 the Russians had already overrun much of Slovakia, and two months later they held over half the country. Czech partisans in Prague and other cities disrupted German communications and harassed German forces in every way they could. On 8 May a concerted Russian offensive attacked from north, south and east, and Prague was liberated the following day. US Army closed the circle on 12 May along a line from Karlovy Vary to Linz. Schörner surrendered with all his forces, five days after the formal surrender of Germany.

Left: The western boundaries of Soviet wartime expansion.
Below: The Allies drive into Czechoslovakia from all directions.
Opposite: Soviet anti-tank gunners.

Fortress Europe Overthrown

The Bomber Offensive on Germany

Allied air raids on Germany began as early as 1940, but it was not until late 1943 that the bombing offensive became systematic and widespread. At that time American 8th Air Force units joined the RAF Bomber Command in force, and several months later an increasing range of escort fighters allowed deep penetration raids over the whole of Germany. RAF Bomber Command concentrated on night bombing of German cities, while the US 8th Air Force, with fewer planes, targeted specific military installations by day.

G R E A T
B R I T A I N

HIGH WYCOMBE
(HQ RAF Bomber Command/
■ HQ US 8 Air Force)
SUNNINGHILL PARK
■ (HQ US 9 Air Force)
BUSHY PARK
■ (HQ US Strategic
Air Force)

F R A

Seine

■1	INDUSTRIAL TARGET
◯1	RAILWAY TARGET
●1	OIL TARGET

| 0 | MILES | | 20 |
| 0 | KILOMETRES | | 300 |

Previous pages: Russian troops in Red Square with captured Nazi banners.
Left: B-24 bombers of the USAAF continue their daylight raids on the Reich.
Above: The ever-expanding operational range of US escort fighters ensured that yet more bombers would hit the target.

Prior to this, several historic raids had been made, including the first '1000-bomber' raid on Cologne (31 May 1942), which destroyed half the target area. Three months later, US 8th Air Force dispatched 12 Flying Fortresses against the marshalling yards near Rouen. Damage was slight, but no American planes were lost, and this raid set the pattern for US concentration on precision bombing in daylight hours.

The night of 18-19 November 1943 brought the first of sixteen major raids on Berlin, where serious damage was inflicted with loss of only nine RAF aircraft. With the arrival of escort fighters in spring of 1944, the 8th Air Force

attacked the Erkner ball-bearing factory in Berlin, disrupting production considerably at a cost of 37 planes. Three weeks later, the RAF struck Nuremberg with almost 800 aircraft, causing some relatively minor damage but losing 95 bombers in the process; 71 others were damaged. The British abandoned area raids on distant objectives after this resounding failure.

The most controversial raid of the war in Europe was that on Dresden (13-14 February 1945). Estimates of civilians killed in this raid ranged from 35,000 to 135,000. Over 1500 acres of the beautiful and historic city – of no military value whatever – were destroyed. The first de-

vastating fire bombing was carried out by 805 Bomber Command aircraft, with the loss of only eight planes. The following day, 8th Air Force bombers overflew the city again.

Strategy: Operation Overlord

At the 1943 Trident Conference in Washington, Allied leaders made their plans for the invasion of Europe – Operation Overlord – during the coming year. France was selected as the target of a cross-Channel assault, with beachheads to be established in Normandy between Cherbourg and Le Havre. This area was within easy reach of fighter bases in southern England and represented the shortest possible route for a massive amphibious operation, excluding the Pas de Calais. Since the Allied invasion was expected in the latter area, the Normandy beaches would be less heavily defended.

The main assault force consisted of the US First and the British Second Armies, with air support from the US 82 and 101 Airborne Divisions and the British 8 Airborne Division. These forces would land right and left of the target beaches to cover the landings. Two artificial ports (called Mulberry Harbors) would be towed across the Channel to permit the landing of tons of supplies before a port could be secured.

Elaborate plans were laid to deceive the Germans into believing that Pas de Calais was the intended target. A dummy headquarters and railroad sidings were built; dozens of sorties were flown over the area; while tons of bombs were dropped west of Le Havre.

German forces guarding the coast of France consisted of Army Group B, commanded by Rommel, and Seventh Army under Dollmann. Hitler had a bad habit of bypassing von Rundstedt, Commander in Chief West, when he issued orders to his Army Group leaders, so the Germans had no effective chain of command in the west. Their position was further jeopardized by topography; destruction of the river crossings on the Loire and the Seine would isolate their forces in Normandy.

Below: Nearly three million men made up the Allied army and supporting forces ready for invasion.
Right: The first landings take place on the Normandy beaches.
Far right: The disposition of opposing German forces.

D-Day

All the careful Allied planning that went into the invasion of France was subject to one imponderable – the weather. June of 1944 opened with unseasonable cold and high winds, which posed serious problems for the strategists. Optimum conditions of moon and tide occurred only a few days each month, and the first week of June comprised such a period.

General Dwight D Eisenhower, Supreme Commander of the operation, decided that the landings must go ahead on schedule. Then a fortunate break in the weather allowed the huge force to launch the largest combined operation in military history on D-Day – 6 June 1944. Three million men, 4600 transports and warships, and almost 10,000 aircraft were involved. General Montgomery

Left: Loading Allied wounded aboard a C-47 Dakota. Note the aircraft's black-and-white invasion stripes, adopted for easy identification.
Below: The invasion beaches.
Right: LCVP landing craft en route to the French coast.

US First Army
(Bradley)

US VII Corps
(Collins)

US V Corps
(Gerow)

US 4 Inf Div

US 1 Inf Div

US 12 Regt

US 22 Regt

US 8 Regt

US 2 Ranger Bn

115 RCT 16 RCT
116 RCT 18 RCT

Cherbourg 13 miles

VALOGNES

MONTEBOURG

709 Inf Div

QUINÉVILLE

ST MARCOUF

RAVENOVILLE
919 Regt

LES DUNES
DE VARREVILLE

ST GERMAIN
DE VARREVILLE

1058 Regt

Planned
assault area

91 Inf Div

Merderet

STE MÈRE ÉGLISE

LA MADELEINE

Uncle

Utah

Victor

US 82
Abn Div

CHEF
DU PONT

Pointe
du Hoe

GRANDCAMP
LES BAINS

Pointe de
la Percée

VIERVILLE SUR MER

Dog

Easy

Omaha

Fox

PONT L'ABBÉ

POUPPEVILLE

ST MARIE-
DU-MONT

ST LAURENT

COLLEVILLE

George

1057 Regt

VIERVILLE

Douve

US 101
Abn Div

STE
HONORINE

6 Para
Regt

ST CÔME-DU-MONT

BRÉVANDS

Part 914 Regt

FORMIGNY

916 Regt

Lessay
9 miles

ST
JORES

CARENTAN

ISIGNY

Part 914 Regt

Aure

TRÉVIÈRES

N 13

30 Regt

Canal de Vire et Taute

Vire

COLOMBIÈRES

352 Inf Div

BLAY

LXXXIV Corps

LITTRY-LA-MINE

SAINTENY

ST JEAN
DE DAYE

St Lô
7 miles

Taute

Forêt
de
Cerisy

Drôme

BALLEROY

BÉRIGNY

Legend

PLANNED AIRBORNE DROPPING AND LANDING ZONES

Utah ASSAULT AREAS

GLIDER LANDINGS

FIRST ASSAULT WAVES

ATTACKS BY BRITISH 6 AIRBORNE DIVISION

HELD BY ALLIES AT 2400 HRS ON D-DAY

ALLIED OBJECTIVE AT 2400 HRS ON D-DAY

RCT US REGIMENTAL COMBAT TEAM

709 Inf Div SITUATION OF GERMAN UNITS AT DAWN ON D-DAY

HELD BY GERMAN TROOPS AT 2400 HRS ON D-DAY

COUNTERATTACKS BY 21 PANZER DIVISION

MAJOR GERMAN GUN BATTERIES

FLOODED AREAS (PRAIRIES MARÉCAGEUSES)

MILES 5 10

KILOMETERS 10 15

'OVERLORD' 6 June 1944
21 Army Group
(Montgomery)

Br Second Army
(Dempsey)

Br XXX Corps
(Bucknall)

Br I Corps
(Crocker)

Br 50 Inf Div
Br 8 Armd Bde

3 Cdn Inf Div
2 Cdn Armd Bde

Br 3 Inf Div
Br 27 Armd Bde

56 Bde

151 Bde

9 Cdn Bde

4 SS Bde

9 Bde

47 RM Cmdos

231 Bde

69 Bde

7 Cdn Bde
8 Cdn Bde

48 RM Cmdos

41 RM Cmdos

185 Bde

1 SS Bde
4 Cmdos

8 Bde

Bay

of

Seine

G o l d

J u n o

S w o r d

How
PORT EN BESSIN

Item

Jig

King

Love *Mike*

Nan

Br 6 Abn Div
5 Para Bde
3 Para Bde

ARROMANCHES

LE HAMEL

LA RIVIÈRE

Bernières
ST AUBIN

HOULGATE

47 RM Cmdos

ASNELLES

COURSEULLES

8 Cdn Bde

LANGRUNE

Oboe

Peter

Queen

Roger

CABOURG
DIVES

231 Bde

LION

726 Regt

56 Bde

151 Bde

CREUILLY

7 Cdn Bde

DOUVRES

9 Bde

OUISTREHAM

MERVILLE

BAYEUX

Seulles

69 Bde

HERMANVILLE

8 Bde

SALLENELLES

ESQUAY

915 Regt

9 Cdn Bde

PÉRIERS

185 Bde

BÉNOUVILLE

Part 736 Regt

VARAVILLE

ST LEGER

Part
736 Regt

BIÉVILLE

RANVILLE

ROBEHOMME

711 Inf Div

LÉBISEY

LE BASSE
DE RANVILLE

Seventh Army
(Dollmann)

BRETTEVILLE
L'ORGUEILLEUSE

21 Pz Div attacks
during afternoon

BURES

Fifteenth Army
(Salmuth)

716 Inf Div

TROARN

Dives

Mue

CARPIQUET

CAEN

XLVII Pz Corps

TILLY-SUR-SEULLES

Airfield

Orne

Falaise

15 miles

FONTENAY

Villers Bocage

3 miles

12 SS Pz Div

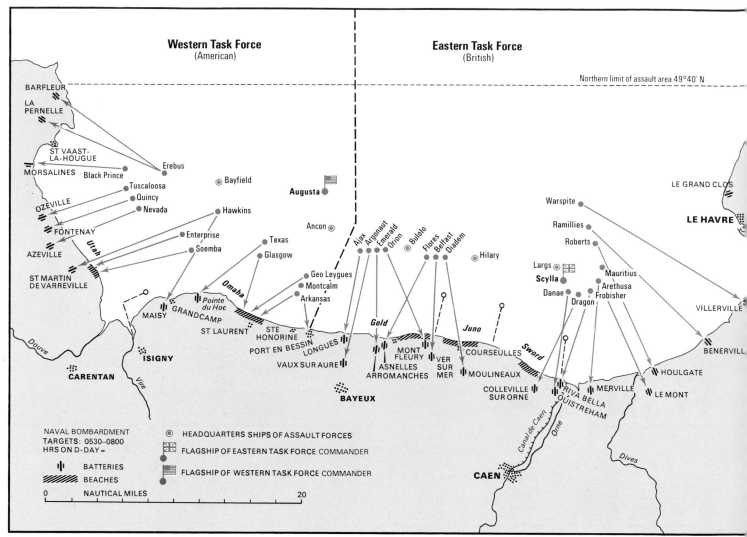

Western Task Force
(American)

Eastern Task Force
(British)

Northern limit of assault area 49°40' N

BARFLEUR

LA PERNELLE

ST VAAST-LA-HOUGUE

MORSALINES

Black Prince

Erebus

OZEVILLE

Tuscaloosa

Quincy

Nevada

Hawkins

FONTENAY

Enterprise

AZEVILLE

Soemba

Utah

ST MARTIN DE VARREVILLE

Bayfield

Augusta

Ancon

Texas

Glasgow

Geo Leygues

Montcalm

Arkansas

Omaha

Pointe du Hoc

MAISY

GRANDCAMP

ST LAURENT

STE HONORINE

PORT EN BESSIN

LONGUES

VAUX SUR AURE

Ajax
Argonaut
Emerald
Orion

Bulolo

Flores

Belfast
Diadem

Hilary

Gold

MONT FLEURY

ASNELLES

ARROMANCHES

VER SUR MER

Juno

COURSEULLES

MOULINEAUX

Warspite

Ramillies

Roberts

Largs

Scylla

Danae

Dragon

Mauritius

Arethusa
Frobisher

Sword

COLLEVILLE SUR ORNE

RIVA BELLA
OUISTREHAM

MERVILLE

MERVILLE

LE GRAND CLOS

LE HAVRE

VILLERVILLE

BENERVILL

HOULGATE

LE MONT

ISIGNY

Douve

CARENTAN

Vire

BAYEUX

Canal de Caen

Orne

Dives

CAEN

NAVAL BOMBARDMENT
TARGETS: 0530–0800
HRS ON D-DAY –

⊙ HEADQUARTERS SHIPS OF ASSAULT FORCES

⚑ FLAGSHIP OF EASTERN TASK FORCE COMMANDER

⚑ FLAGSHIP OF WESTERN TASK FORCE COMMANDER

▮ BATTERIES

▨ BEACHES

0   NAUTICAL MILES   20

commanded ground forces, Admiral Ramsay co-ordinated naval operations and Air Marshal Leigh-Mallory was charged with air support. Preparatory air attacks were particularly important in view of the shortage of paratroop-transport aircraft and the comparative strength of opposing ground forces – some half a million men of the German Seventh Army.

Hitler himself contributed to Allied success by misusing the advice of two of his ablest generals to produce a compromise scheme that seriously hampered the German defense. Field Marshal von Rundstedt, Commander in Chief West, wanted to form a strong central reserve until the true Allied plan was known and then use it to repel the invasion, keeping beach defenses to a minimum. Rommel, commanding German armies in northern France and the Low Countries, cautioned that Allied air power would prevent Rundstedt's reserve from coming into action and recommended that the Allies should be defeated on the beaches before they could reach full strength. Hitler's compromise – strongly influenced by inflated reports of Allied manpower – neither strengthened the beaches sufficiently nor allowed for the flexible use of Rundstedt's reserve.

Five beaches were targeted for the Allied landings, code-named Utah, Omaha, Gold, Juno and Sword. At 2:00 AM on 6 June, US and British airborne forces descended on their objectives and consolidated a position within the hour. Tactical surprise was complete, thanks to the months of painstaking work by the deception team. An hour later, aerial bombardment of the beaches began, soon followed by fire from the 600 warships that had assembled off the coast. At 6:30 AM the first waves went ashore, US First Army on Utah and Omaha Beaches and British Second Army on Gold, Juno and Sword. Real problems were encountered only on Omaha, where landing forces were deprived of full amphibious tank support by rough seas. They were pinned down on the beach for hours, but managed to fight their way out to the coast road by nightfall. Within 24 hours, the Allies had achieved almost all their objectives for D-Day.

Above: Disposition of Allied bombardment vessels on D-Day.
Top right: LST landing ships disgorge men and matériel.
Right: A convoy of US Coast Guard landing craft (LCI) head for Normandy.

The Anvil Landings in Southern France

US and British leaders disagreed on the necessity of landing forces in southern France to support Operation Overlord on the Normandy coast. The Americans argued that such landings could open the much-needed port of Marseilles and draw off German troops from the north, but this could be done only by transferring troops from Italy. British leaders saw vast untapped potential in the Italian campaign and argued for pouring men and munitions into Italy to facilitate an advance over the Alps toward Vienna and the Danube. Stalin had his own vested interest in an Anglo-American effort as far west of Russia as possible, and he enlisted US President Franklin D Roosevelt's support. It was the American plan that prevailed.

Operation Anvil was postponed from June 1944 – simultaneous with D-Day – to 15 August, due to a shortage of landing craft. On that date US Seventh Army made landings between Toulon and Cannes. Ninety-four thousand men and 11,000 vehicles came ashore with fewer than 200 casualties: all of southern France was defended by only eight German divisions. The French II Corps, under General de Lattre de Tassigny, then advanced toward Toulon and Marseilles, while US elements closed in on the German Nineteenth Army, taking 15,000 prisoners. De Lattre captured both his objectives, and US Lieutenant General Alexander Patch fought his way up the Rhône Valley to make contact with Patton's Third Army on 12 September. The newly formed French First Army then combined with US Seventh to form the US 6 Army Group under Lieutenant General Jacob Devers to drive into Germany on the right of the Allied line.

The Allied Breakout from Normandy

It took over half the summer for Allied forces to extend their initial beach-heads well into Normandy, where Rommel had been reinforced from the south of France. Montgomery adhered to his original campaign plan and made

Opposite bottom: Anvil, Overlord and the British plan over which they prevailed.
Left: US troops drive the Germans from southern France.
Below: Patton's Third Army pours through the Avranches Gap and sweeps south toward the Loire.
Inset: Pursuit and defeat of German forces at the Atlantic coast.

slow but steady progress (although not enough to satisfy his critics, who were numerous). By 27 July (D+50), the Cotentin Peninsula was in Allied hands. Patton's US Third Army broke through the Avranches gap into Brittany and central France, and US, British and Canadian Forces attacked south and east in early August.

Hitler responded with orders for immediate counterattacks, which failed to contain the Allied advance. Both von Rundstedt and Rommel had been replaced in early July, and their successor, von Kluge, was pulled out on 25 August after four Allied armies pursued him to

the Seine crossings. Patton's armor reached the Seine at Fontainbleu on the same day that US and Canadian forces closed the gap at Falaise, cutting off the escape of German Seventh and Fifth Panzer Armies. By this time, 10,000 German soldiers had died and 50,000 more had been taken prisoner.

The US XV Corps established a bridge-head downstream of Paris as soon as it reached the Seine, and five days later, on 25 August, the French capital was liberated. Kluge had succeeded in salvaging much of Army Group B, but his command was turned over to General Model by way of thanks.

Above: US armor crosses the Siegfried
Line en route for Germany.
Left: The escape route for the Fifth and
Seventh German armies ended at Falaise.
Above right: Reclaiming France and the
Low Countries, summer 1944.
Right: German soldiers pictured on the
long march to captivity.

Advance to Antwerp

The remarkable achievement of Allied operations in Normandy should have been followed up, according to Montgomery and other strategists, by a narrow-front thrust into Germany to end the war in 1944. Eisenhower, who assumed direct control of ground forces in September as a function of supreme command, favored a slow advance in line by all Allied forces. The critical issue in August 1944 was that of supply: the logistics of providing food, fuel and other necessities to four Allied armies now 300 miles from the Normandy coast had become unworkable. A port was needed desperately.

Montgomery, Bradley and other narrow-front proponents argued for supplying part of the Allied force abundantly and sending it through Belgium to encircle the Ruhr and advance on Berlin at top speed. Eisenhower held out for a more cautious advance that did not underestimate the power of German armies still in the field despite their losses – 700,000 men since D-Day. There was far less risk in this approach, both strategically and politically. The disadvantage was in dragging out the war until 1945, which meant that the Russians would have time to establish their armies far west of their borders.

The Canadian First Army seized several small French Channel ports, and on 4 September the Allies captured the large port of Antwerp with its facilities almost intact. But failure to consolidate their grip on this valuable harbor immediately resulted in loss of control of the Scheldt Estuary, its seaward approach, to the Germans.

Arnhem and the Drive to the Rhine

Below: The Allies advance.
Bottom: The two tactical alternatives – a strong thrust (left) and the more cautious advance actually adopted (right).
Right: Operation Market Garden, mounted against four key river bridges.
Far right: British airborne forces ran into trouble at Arnhem.
Below right: US troops bridge the Rhine.

Once Belgium was liberated, the Allies sought to secure a continuous northernward advance by capturing a series of four bridges at key canal and river crossings. This would create a corridor through the Netherlands for a swing around the northern end of Germany's West Wall defenses (which were by no means as strong as the Allies supposed). Montgomery planned to drop three airborne divisions near the bridges at Veghel, Grave, Nijmegen and Arnhem in an operation that was hastily assembled under the code name of 'Market Garden.'

The 17 September landings at Veghel and Grave by US 101 and 82 Airborne Divisions were successful, and British XXX Corps linked up with these forces the following day. They captured the bridge at Nijmegen on 20 September, but were unable to make further progress. At Arnhem, British 1 Airborne Division was in desperate straits as a result of landing too far from the bridge in a strongly defended area. Only one battalion reached the objective, where it was immediately cut off, and the rest of the division was surrounded. Only 2200 survivors made it back to British lines; 7000 others remained behind to be killed, wounded or captured.

The port of Antwerp was still useless to the Allies on account of German forces in the Scheldt Estuary, which was not cleared until early November. Then Bradley's 12 Army Group was enlarged by the arrival of the US Ninth Army, and 6 Army Group pushed through the Vosges Mountains to the German border. By 15 December 1944, the Allies were poised to cross the Rhine.

OPERATION 'MARKET GARDEN'

17 Sept 1944
Strong German forces block routes to bridge. PM, 2 Bn captures bridge but is cut off. Remnants of division withdraw across river to British lines on 25 Sept

20 Sept
Nijmegen bridge captured in joint attack by US paratroops and Br XXX Corps

PM 17 Sept
Bridge captured. Br XXX Corps links up with paratroops at 0820 19 Sept

17 Sept
All bridges captured. Br XXX Corps links up with paratroops PM 18 Sept

ALLIED AIRBORNE LANDINGS AT MID-DAY 17 SEPT 1944

MAIN GERMAN COUNTERATTACKS

Germany's Last Throw: The Battle of the Bulge

As they prepared to cross the Rhine into Germany, the Allies discounted any possibility that the Germans would launch a last-ditch offensive. In fact, Hitler had scraped together his last reserves and ordered them to break through the Allied front in the Ardennes, split US and British forces, and drive on to Antwerp to cut off Allied supplies. Twenty-four German divisions, 10 of them armored, were involved in this bold offensive, which came dangerously close to succeeding.

Since they lacked air cover, the Germans were fortunate that low cloud and a heavy snowfall concealed their move-

ments through the Ardennes. On 16 December eight Panzer Divisions appeared seemingly from nowhere to fall upon the US VIII Corps in the first encounter of a six-week struggle. The British would call it the Battle of the Ardennes, the Americans the Battle of the Bulge.

German tactical surprise was complete, and additional confusion spread through the US lines when English-speaking German soldiers in Allied uniforms (carefully coached in American slang) made their presence known. Eisenhower was forced to commit his reserves to the bulge in his line, including airborne divisions that were still resting

from Operation Market Garden. The US 101 Airborne Division arrived in Bastogne only to be trapped on 20 December, as German forces prepared to head for the Meuse.

Then the Allies rallied to mount a concerted attack on the German salient by Hodges' US First Army and Patton's Third Army. Montgomery took charge of all Allied units north of the bulge, and Bradley assumed command in the south. By Christmas Eve, the Ardennes Offensive was grinding to a halt for lack of fuel. The Germans were unable to overrun Allied fuel dumps, and stiffening opposition completed their undoing. The last major Luftwaffe effort of the war, against airfields in France, Belgium and Holland, had no effect on the punishing aerial attacks that supported Allied ground forces in the Ardennes.

Hitler's gamble had failed long before 7 February 1945, when the salient was finally eliminated. With it went the last German forces that might have stopped the Russian onslaught now preparing to fall upon the German homeland.

Above: Hitler's plan to split the British and US forces by making for Antwerp.
Left: The Panzers break out into the Ardennes.
Above right: An Allied supply line rolls through Bastogne in January 1945 after its relief.
Right: Bastogne under siege in December 1944; the US 101st Airborne Division defends the perimeter.

Crossing the Rhine

Right: Crossing the Rhine.

Below: A US Army half-track guards against air attack at Remagen, a key Rhine crossing-point captured on 7 March.
Bottom: German prisoners taken in the drive to the Rhine east of the Roer river, February 1945.
Right: Crossing the Rhine.

The Rhine River was the greatest water obstacle in Western Europe, and no Allied leader expected to cross it with impunity. Not until early March 1945 were sufficient forces in place to attempt the capture of a vital bridge. This was achieved on 7 March in a brilliant stroke by men of Hodges' US First Army, who seized the Ludendorff railroad bridge at Remagen intact, then established a bridgehead with bewildering speed. Valuable as this was, additional crossings had to be secured both up- and downstream of Remagen before it could be exploited.

On 22 March, US Third Army made a second crossing at Nierstein, soon followed by others at points from Nijmegen to Mannheim. Wiesbaden was captured on 27 March; the day before, US Seventh Army had crossed near Worms to link up with Patton's Third Army on the east bank. From 31 March onward, the French First Army began to force crossings south of Mannheim, and within a week's time the Germans had lost all their positions on the Rhine's east bank.

The Drive into Germany

The Allied advance through Germany from the Rhine to the Elbe met bitter opposition at several points where determined German leaders still commanded veteran troops. But for the most part, resistance was minimal; German units lacked food, fuel, ammunition and leadership by this time, and many welcomed the opportunity to surrender to the Americans rather than face the Russians.

Eisenhower had focused most of his attacks in the south, due partly to reports that the Germans would retreat to an 'Alpine Redoubt' whose unspecified location was largely in Hitler's mind. First and Third Armies had crossed the Rhine south of Aachen with unexpected ease, and German communications had broken down almost entirely. There is no doubt that the Allies could have reached both Berlin and Prague in April 1945, but US commitments to the Soviet Union mandated a halt on the Elbe. As the Allied armies advanced through Germany to link up with the Russians, they discovered Belsen, Buchenwald and other camps whose infamies had been rumored but not fully known until that time. Anger against the Nazi régime hardened with every appalling discovery, as films and pictures from the camps began to reach the world.

The Fall of Berlin

Below: The victors and the defeated. Soviet troops enter Berlin, May 1945.
Below left: The partition of Berlin.
Bottom: Occupied Germany as it appeared at the war's end.
Right: As Berlin falls, the war in Europe comes to an end.

By mid April 1945, Soviet forces along the Oder were ready to advance on Berlin. Konev's 1 Ukrainian Front and Zhukov's 1 Belorussian Front (some 2,500,000 men) faced a million German defenders in strong positions on the Oder's west bank. The desperate Germans were keenly aware of the consequences should the Russians break through, and they were prepared to fight as never before.

The opening Russian bombardment employed a record-breaking concentration of one gun per 13 feet of front. It was a fitting prelude to one of the most ferocious bouts of the war. Only two small bridgeheads were achieved in the first two days (16-18 April), but deeper penetrations were made in the following 48 hours. By 20 April, German resistance on the Oder was shattered, and five days later the two Russian forces had encircled the city to meet on its west side. It was on the same day, 25 April, that US and Soviet forces made contact on the Elbe at Torgau.

Berlin contained 2,000,000 civilians and a garrison of some 30,000. Its rudimentary defenses were wholly unequal to the forces massed against it, but the city resisted to the last. From 26 April to 2 May, fighting raged in the streets, as the two Russian armies moved in from north and south to meet across the Charlottenberg Chaussee. Before they made contact, the Reichstag fell (30 April), and Hitler died by his own hand, naming Admiral Karl Dönitz as his successor.

On 4 May 1945, General Montgomery accepted Germany's unconditional surrender, and three days later the war in Europe was formally at an end. The victors divided both Germany and Berlin (which was deep in the Soviet sector) into four zones each, to be controlled by the four major Allies. The stage was set for Soviet hegemony in Eastern Europe, the Cold War, emerging nationalism among former subject peoples around the world, and the precarious new balance of power that persists to this day.

BALTIC SEA

Rügen

STRALSUND
RIBNITZ

ROSTOCK

GRIEFSWALD

DEMMIN

PEENEMÜNDE

Usedom

SWINEMÜNDE

Stettiner Haff

19A

UECKERMUNDE

WISMAR

British Second Army

SCHWERIN

70A

7 May

GUSTROW

WAREN

Müritz

FRIEDLAND

Third Pz Army

2SA

NEUBRANDENBURG

PACEWALK

STETTIN

2 Belorussian Front (Rokossovsky)

attacks AM 20 April

2SA

STARGARD

PARCHIM

Army Group Vistula
(Heinrici, then Tippelskirch
acting for Student)

LUDWIGSLUST

49A

NEUSTRELITZ

PRENZLAU

65A

70A

DÖMITZ

LENZEN

PRITZWALK

WITTSTOCK

TEMPLIN

SCHWEDT

49A

ANGERMUNDE

61A

WITTENBERGE

ZEHDENICK

NEURUPPIN

**Operational
Group Steiner**

Oder-Havel Canal

EBERSWALDE

61A

Pol1A

1 Belorussian Front (Zhukov)

attacks 0500 hrs, 16 April

Warta

US Ninth Army

Pol1A

Rhinkanal

ORANIENBURG

2 GTA

47A

3SA

5SA

KUSTRIN

18 Apr

STENDAL

RATHENOW

47A

BERNAU

PROTZEL

STRAUSBERG

8GA

1 GTA

3A

TANGERMÜNDE

KETZIN

BERLIN

5SA

1 GTA

SEELOW

69A

FRANKFURT an der Oder

GENTHIN

Havel

POTSDAM

8GA

FÜRSTENWALDE

3A

BRANDENBURG

28A

3A

69A

33A

BURG

3GTA

BEELITZ

DOSSEN

BEESKOW

EISENHÜTTENSTADT

Uder

MAGDEBURG

Twelfth Army

69A

BELZIG

4GTA

MARKISCH
BUCHHOLZ

**Ninth Army
& part
Fourth Pz
Army**

33A

LUCKENWALDE

BARUTH

GUBEN

ZERBST

JÜTERBOG

LÜBBEN

Spree

US First Army

BERNBURG

WITTENBERG

13A

LUCKAU

3
GA

1 Ukrainian Front (Konev)

attacks 0615 hrs, 16 April

Saale

DESSAU

COTTBUS
22 Apr

FORST

3GTA

SCHLIEBEN

FINSTERWALDE

US front
25 April

HERZBERG

SPREMBERG

TRIEBEL

13A

4GTA

TORGAU

5GA

**Army Group
Center** (Schörner)

**Fourth Pz
Army**

5GA

Neisse

HALLE

EILENBURG

25 April 1945
US and Russian
forces make
contact

ELSTERWALDE

HOYERSWERDE

28A

LEIPZIG

Mulde

18 Apr

Elbe

RIESA

GROSSENHAIN

KAMENZ

NIESKY

Pol2A

52A

COLDITZ

MEISSEN

Pol2A

BAUTZEN

GÖRLITZ

RADEBERG

DRESDEN

Seventeenth Army

MILES 0 — 40
KILOMETERS 0 — 60

FRONT LINES
15 APRIL 1945
18 APRIL
25 APRIL
6 MAY
GERMAN DEFENSE LINES
GERMAN POCKETS
GERMAN COUNTERATTACKS
ANGLO-AMERICAN ATTACKS
ANGLO-AMERICAN FRONTS AT DATES SHOWN

Index

Index of maps

Alam Halfa 57
Anzio landings 117, 118
Arakan battles 140
Arctic convoys 39
Ardennes, German breakthrough in 182
Arnhem 181
Atlantic, Battle of
  to May 1940 34
  June 1940 to March 1941 35
  April to December 1941 36
  January to July 1942 37
  Bismarck episode 38
  August 1942 to May 1943 40
  June 1943 to May 1945 41
Avranches breakthrough 177

Bataan Peninsula 103
Belgium
  German and Allied plans 18
  disposition of forces in 1939 19
  overrun 22, 23
  Allied advance to Antwerp, 1944 179
Berlin, partition of 188
  encirclement of 189
Bismarck episode 38
Bougainville 125
Britain, Battle of 27
Burma, invasion of 107
  Arakan battles, 1942-43 140
  Operation Ha-Go, 1944 140
  Allied Northern and Southern Groups, 1943 142
  drive to Mandalay, 1944-45 145
  Meiktila and Mandalay, 1945 146

Calais 24
China, Japanese occupation of 147
Convoy PQ-17 39
Coral Sea, Battle of 122
Corregidor 103
Crimea 161
Czechoslovakia, Allied drive into 164

Dunkirk 23, 24
Dutch East Indies 106

East Prussia 162
Eastern Front
  planned thrusts to Moscow, Kiev and Leningrad 68
  relative strengths and dispositions, June 1941 69
  Operation Barbarossa 71
  attack on Leningrad 73
  the Ukraine 74, 161
  advance on Moscow 75, 76
  Soviet counter-offensive, December 1941 76
  Soviet advance to April 1942 77
  drive to the Volga 150
  defense of Stalingrad 152
  Kursk offensive 154
  front lines, 1943 156
  front lines to Spring 1944 161
  front lines, January to May 1945 163
  Warsaw to the Oder 163
  encirclement of Berlin 189
El Alamein, First Battle of 55
  Second Battle of 58, 59
Europe, in 1939 12
  pre-1914 and 1919 boundaries 81

Falaise pocket 178
Finland
  Mannerheim Line 66
  Soviet penetration of, 1939-40 66, 67
  front line in 1941 72
France
  defensive positions in 1939 19
  overrun 22, 25
  divided 23
  defense of Calais 24
  Italian incursions 25
  Allied landings in Normandy 170, 172-3
  German dispositions in 1944 171
  Allied landings in South, 176
  breakthrough at Avranches 177
  Falaise pocket 178
  advance to Antwerp 179

Gazala 46
Germany
  expansion by August 1939 12, 82
  in 1939-40 16, 83
  in 1940 22
  by 1942 84
  thrust into Poland 14
  advance in Denmark and Norway 16
  Siegfried Line, 1939 19
  advance into Low Countries 20
  thrust to the Meuse 21
  advance through Belgium and France 22, 23
  invasion of Yugoslavia 29
  through Libya into Egypt 44, 45
  contraction and defeat of 92, 93
  bomber offensive against 169
  Allied drive into 187
  Allied Occupation Zones 188
  Soviet advance to Berlin 189

Greece
  Italian attacks and counter-offensives 30, 31
  British evacuation of 31
Guadalcanal 125, 126

Hong Kong 102

Imphal 144
Italy
  expansion of 82, 83
  Allied landings in 110, 111
  Gustav Line 113, 114, 115
  Allied advance in 117, 119
  Anzio landings 117, 118
  Gothic Line 119
Iwo Jima 133

Japan
  1941 sphere of influence 86-7
  1941-42 expansion in Pacific 88-9
  limit of expansion, August 1942 90
  reversals in Pacific, 1944-45 94
  occupied territories, December 1941 98-9
  bombing of 136-7

Kohima 143
Kursk 154

Leningrad, defense of 73, 158
  relief of 158
Leyte, land battles for 130
Leyte Gulf, Battle of 131
Luzon, Japanese landings on 104
  recapture of 132

Malaya, Japanese conquest of 101
Malta 53
Mandalay 146
Mannerheim Line 66
Matapan, Battle of 49
Mediterranean, naval war in 49, 52-3
Meiktila 146
Mersa Matruh 54
Midway, Battle of 123
Moscow, advance on 75, 76

New Guinea 124, 125
  US landings on 127
North Africa
  German advance into Egypt, March/April 1941 44, 45, 54
  Tobruk 44, 46, 47, 48
  German advance to Gazala and Tobruk 46
  First Battle of El Alamein 55
  Alam Halfa 57
  Second Battle of El Alamein 58, 59
  Operation Torch 60
  Allied advance into Tunisia 61, 62, 63
  Eighth Army advance, El Alamein to Mareth Line 62-3

Okinawa 134
Operation Anvil 176
Operation Barbarossa 71
Operation Market Garden 181
Operation Overlord 170, 176
  landing beaches 172-3
  Allied naval dispositions 174
Operation Torch 60

Pacific
  Japanese sphere of influence 1941 86
  Japanese expansion in 88, 90, 98
  Japanese containment in 94
Pearl Harbor 99
Philippine Islands 128
  conquest of 103, 104
  liberation of 130, 131, 132
Philippine Sea, Battle of 128
Poland
  German thrust into 14
  Russian advance into 14
  partition of 14
  Soviet reoccupation 163

Rhine, Allied advance to 180
  crossing of 185
Rhineland, 1936 reoccupation 12, 82

Sicily 110
Singapore 101
Solomon Islands 124-5
Soviet Union
  disposition of forces, 1941 69
  defense of Leningrad 73, 158
  December 1941 counter-offensive 76
  gains to April 1942 77
  gains to November 1943 156
  gains to Spring 1944 161
  wartime expansion 164
Stalingrad 150, 152
Sudetenland 12

Taranto, attack on 49
Tassafaronga, Battle of 126
Tobruk 44, 46, 47, 48
Tunisia, Allied advance into 61

Ukraine, German capture of 74
  Soviet reoccupation 161

Yugoslavia, German invasion of 29

General Index

Page numbers in italics refer to illustrations

ABDA Command 106
Alam Halfa, Battle of 56-7
Albania 30
Alexander, General Sir Harold 56, 62, 107
Algiers 60, *60*
Allied army formations
  6 Army Group 176, 180
  12 Army Group 180
  15 Army Group 180
  see also British Army, French Army, United States Army

Altmark, SS 16
Anglo-German Naval Agreement 14
Anglo-German rivalry 6
Antwerp 179, 180
Anzio 117
Arakan 140
Ardennes 18, 20, 182-3
Arizona, USS, battleship *78-9*, 100
Ark Royal, HMS, carrier 38
Arnhem 180, *181*
Arnim, General Jurgen von 62
Atlantic, Battle of *32-7*, 34-8, 40-1, *41*, 92
atomic bomb, 136, *136*
Auchinleck, General Sir Claude 54, 56
Australia 15, 91, 122, 127
Australian armed forces 30, 91, 127
  7 Australian Division 44
  8 Australian Division 44

Barham, HMS, battleship *50-1*
Bastogne 182, *183*
Bataan 103, *105*
Belgium 18, 20, 21, 80, 179
Berlin 7, *93*, 169, 179, 186, 188, *188*
Bir Hacheim 47
Bismarck, German battleship 38
'blitzkrieg' 14, 16, 17, 20, 29, 82
Blücher, German cruiser 16
Bock, General Fedor von 68, 150
Bougainville 125
Bradley, General Omar N 179, 180
Britain, Battle of *26*, 26-8, 82
British Army
  in France/Belgium, 1940 18, 20, 22, *24*, 82
  in United Kingdom, 1940 26
  in Greece 30
  in North Africa 44, 46-8, *48*, 54, *55*, 56, *56*, 58, 60, 62
  in Far East 101-2, *102*, 107, 140-6, *141*
  in Sicily/Italy 110-2, 114, 119
  in Northwest Europe 174, 177, 179-80
  First Canadian Army 179
  Second Army 170, 174
  Eighth Army 46-8, 54, 56, 58, 62, 110, 111, 112, 119
  Fourteenth Army 143, 145
  IV Corps 144
  V Corps 62
  X Corps 58, 111
  XIII Corps 47, 58
  XV Corps 140, 143, 145
  XXX Corps 58, 180
  XXXIII Corps 143
  New Zealand Corps 114
  1st Airborne Division 180, *181*
  2nd Division 143, 144
  2nd Armored Division 44
  5th Indian Division 140
  7th Armored Division 56
  7th Indian Division 140
  8th Airborne Division 170
  8th Australian Division 44
  9th Australian Division 54
  11th Indian Division 101
  14th Indian Division 140
  3rd Indian Brigade 44
  4th Brigade 143
  5th Brigade 143
  22nd Armored Brigade *55*, 56
British Empire 6, 7
Bryansk 70
Buckner, General Simon Bolivar 134
Bulgaria, Bulgarians 29, 30
Bulge, Battle of the 182
Bunker Hill, USS, carrier *128*
Burma *9*, 89, *106*, 107, 140-6
Burrough, Rear Admiral HM 52
Busch, General Ernest 162

Cairo, HMS, cruiser 52
Calais 18, 22
Canadian armed forces 177
  First Canadian Army 179

Cape Matapan, Battle of 49
Casablanca 60
Cassin, USS *100*
Caucasian oilfields 150
Cavallero, Marshal Ugo 111
Chamberlain, Neville 6-7, 13
Chennault, General Claire 107, 147, *147*
Chiang Kai-shek 140, *147*
China 87, 140, 147
Chindit operations 142
Chinese armed forces 107, 147
Christison, General Sir Philip 140
Chuikov, Marshal Vasili *151*
Churchill, Winston 6, 22, 36, 56, 101, 110, 142
Clark, General Mark 111, 117, 119
concentration camps 12
convoys 34, 35, 36, 37, 39, 40-1, 83
  to Malta 52
  to Russia 39
Coral Sea, Battle of 95, 122, 123
Corregidor Island 103
Coventry, bombing of *28*
Crace, Rear Admiral John 122
Crete 30
Crimea 70, 76, 77, 156, 160
Cruewell, General Ludwig 47
Cunningham, Admiral Sir Andrew 49
Czechoslovakia 7, 13, 80, 162, 164

Danzig 80
de Gaulle, General Charles 22
Denmark 16, 17
Devers, Lieutenant General Jacob 176
Dollman, General 170
Dönitz, Admiral Karl 188
Doolittle raid on Tokyo 89, 122, *137*
Doorman, Rear Admiral Karel 106
Dorsetshire, HMS, cruiser 38
Dowding, Air Chief Marshal Sir Hugh 26
Downes, USS, *100*
Dunkirk 7, 21, 22, 24, *24*, 26, 82
Dutch East Indies 89, 106

Eagle, HMS, carrier 52
East Prussia 13
Eastern Solomons, Battle of 124
Eisenhower, General Dwight D, *53*, 60, 171, 179, 182, 186
El Alamein 56, 60
  First Battle of 54
  Germans retreat from *42-3*
  Second Battle of 58, *58*
Enterprise, USS, carrier 123
Exeter, HMS, cruiser 106

Falaise pocket 177
Finland 66, 72
  armed forces of 66, *73*
  German alliance with 66, 70, 72
Fiume, Italian cruiser 49
Fletcher, Vice-Admiral Frank 95, 122, 124
Foch, Marshal Ferdinand 12
Foresight, HMS, destroyer 52
France 13, 14, 15, 16, 18, 34, 80, 176
  1944-45 campaign in 170-7, 179
  and Finland 66
  fall of 20-2, 26, 34
  Free French 22
  Vichy France 22, 60
French Army 18, 22
  troops of *24*
  First Army 176, 184
  Seventh Army 20
  II Corps 176
  French Expeditionary Corps 114
French fleet 34
French Indochina 87
French North Africa, invasion of 40, 60, *60-1*
Furious, HMS, carrier 52

Gamelin, General Maurice 18
Gazala 47, 48

German air force 13, 14, 22, 26-8, *28*, 48, 52, 153, 162, 182
German army 12, 82
  in Poland 14, *15*, 82
  in Scandinavia 16-7, 82
  in France/Belgium, 1940 18, 20-1, 82
  in Yugoslavia 29
  in Greece 30, *30*
  in North Africa *42-3*, 44, 46-8, *47*, 54, 56-7, *57*, 58, 60, 62
  on Eastern Front *64-5*, 68, 70, 72-4, 76, 152-6, *153*, 158, 160, *160-1*, 162, 164
  in Sicily/Italy 110-1, 114, 117, *118*, 119
  in North-West Europe, 1944-45 170, 174, 176, 177, *178*, 179, 180, 182-3, *184, 184*, 186
  troops of, in Paris *1, 23*
  Army Group North 68, 73, 158
  Army Group Centre 68, 70, 162
  Army Group South 68, 70, 150, 156
  Army Group A 150, 156, 160
  Army Group B 150
  Army Group North Ukraine 160
  Army Group B (France) 170, 177
  First Pz Army 160
  Second Army 29, 70, 162
  Second Pz Army 76
  Fourth Pz Army 154
  Fifth Pz Army 177
  Sixth Army 160
  Seventh Army 170, 174
  Eighth Army 160
  Ninth Army 154
  Tenth Army 112, 117, 119
  Twelfth Army 29
  Fourteenth Army 119
  Seventeenth Army 156, 160, 177
  Nineteenth Army 176
  First Panzer Group 29
  Second Panzer Group 70
  Third Panzer Group 74, 76
  Fourth Panzer Group 70
  Afrika Korps 46-7, *47*, 48, 56
  5th Light Division 44
  15th Panzer Division 56
  21st Panzer Division 48, 58
  Waffen-SS 73
German navy 16, 17, 26, 162
Germany 85, 150
  Allied advance into 179, 184-6, 188
  and invasion of Russia 68, 84
  and Versailles Treaty 80-1
  bombing offensive against 92, *93*, *168*, 168-9
  Democratic Republic of 7
  expansion in, 1939-42 82-4
  pre-war ascendancy of 6-7, 13
Gurkha troops 142
Gort, Field Marshal Viscount 53
Gothic Line 119
Goto, Rear Admiral 122
Great Britain
  and Czechoslovakia 7, 13
  and Finland 66
  and Poland 14, 15
  and the Empire 6, 7
  Battle of Britain 26
  early strategy in war 16, 18
  prewar German rivalry with 6
  prewar reaction to Hitler 6, 7, 13
Greece 29, 30, 49, 83
Guadalcanal 95, 124-5, *124-5*
Guam 128
Guderian, General Heinz 70
Gustav Line 111, 112, 114-5, 117
Guzzoni, General Alfredo 110

Halfaya Pass 44
Halifax, Lord 6
Halsey, Admiral William 130
Herr, General Traugott 119
Hipper, German cruiser 39
Hiroshima 136
Hiryu, Japanese carrier 123
Hitler, Adolf 6, *13, 112*
  'Alpine Redoubt' of 186

ambitions and aggression of 7, 13, 14
  and Allied invasion 170, 174, 177
  and Ardennes offensive 182, 183
  and Eastern Front 70, 76, 110
  and North Africa 48, 60, 84
  and Stalingrad 150, 153
  and submarine warfare 34
  and Versailles Treaty 12, 13
  Balkan takeover 29, 30, 84
  cancellation of Sealion 28
  concern over Italy 110, 111
  death of 188
  decision to attack Russia 66, 68, 84, 150
  military interference by 18, 21, 58, 150, 170, 174
  mistakes Allies' desire for peace 16, 26
  'No retreat' orders 58, 156
  replaces Kleist, Manstein 160
  replaces Kluger 177
  success in Scandinavia 16-7
  underestimates Russians 66, 77
Hodges, General Courtney 182, 184
Holland 18, 20
  armed forces of *21*
Holland, Vice-Admiral Lancelot 38
Hong Kong 102, *102*
Hood, HMS, battlecruiser 38
Hornet, USS, carrier 123
Horrocks, General Sir Brian *58*
Houston, USS, cruiser 106

Iida, General 140
Illustrious, HMS, carrier 49
Imphal 140, 143-4, 145
Indian troops 140, 142
Indomitable, HMS, carrier 52
Ino, Genral Matsuichi 95
Inouye, Admiral Shigeyoshi 122
island-hopping strategy 91
Italian air force 52
Italian navy 49
Italian troops 22, 29, 30, 83, 110
  in Italy 119
  in North Africa 44, 54, 58, *59*, 83
  on Eastern Front *2-3*
Italy 7, 30, 34, 92, 110, 155
  campaign in 110-9, 176
Iwo Jima 133, *133*, 136

Japan 94
  and China 147
  bombing of *95*, 136, *137*
  prewar attitude of 7, 9, 87
  war strategy 89, 106, 122, 123
Japanese army 8, 89, 91, *106*, 130, 132, 133, *141*
  Fourteenth Army 103
  Fifteenth Army 107, 143, 144, 145
  Twentyfifth Army 101
  Thirtysecond Army 134
  China Expeditionary Army 147
  in Burma 140, 142, 144-5
Japanese navy 89
  First Mobile Fleet 128
Java Sea, Battle of 106

Kamikaze attacks 131, 134
Karelian Isthmus 66, 72
Kasserine, Battle of 62
Katamura, Lieutenant General Shihachi 145
Kenya, HMS, cruiser 52
Kesselring, Field Marshal Albert 60, 111, 112, 114, 119
Kharkov 156
Kiev 70, 74, 156
Kincaid, Admiral Thomas 130
King George V, HMS, battleship 38
Kleist, General Paul von 29, 160
Klopper, General 48
Kluge, General Gunther von 177
Kobe, Japan *95*
Kohima 143-4, 145
Konev, Marshal Ivan *162*, 188
Krueger, General Walter 130
Küchler, General 158

Kuribayashi, Major General Tadamichi 133
Kurita, Admiral Takeo 131
Kursk 92, 110, 154-5, *155*

Lake Ladoga 72, 73, 158
Lattre de Tassigny, General Jean de 176
League of Nations 12-3, 66, 87
Leahy, Admiral W D *80*
Leeb, General Wilhelm von 68, 73
Leigh-Mallory, Air Marshal Trafford 174
Lemelsen, General Joachim 119
Leningrad 68, 70, 72, 73, 76, 77, 158, *159*, 160
Lexington, USS, carrier 99, 122, 123, *129*
Leyte 130, *130*, 131, *132*
Leyte Gulf, Battle of 128, 130-1
Lithuania 80
Littorio, Italian battleship 49
London, air raids on *26, 28*
Lucas, Major General John 117
Lütjens, Vice-Admiral Günther 38
Lützow, pocket battleship 16
Luzon 103-4, 131-2

MacArthur, General Douglas *80*, 91, 103, *127*, 130, 134
Mackensen, General 117
Maginot Line 18, 82
Malaya 9, 89, 101, *101*, 102
Manchester, HMS, cruiser 52
Manchuria 87
Mandalay 145
Mannerheim, Marshal Carl von 72
Mannerheim Line 66, *72*
Manstein, General Erich von 18, 20, 156, 160
Mao Tse-tung 147
Mareth Line 62
Marianas Islands *120-1*, 127, 128, 136
Marseilles 176
Marshall, General George C 147
Mediterranean 49, 52
Meiktila 146
Memel 80
Merrill's Marauders *144*
Mersa Matruh 54
Messe, Marshal Giovanni 62
Midway 124
  Battle of 95, 123, 124
Mitscher, Vice-Admiral Marc 128
Model, Field Marshal Walther 158, 160, 162, 177
Monte Cassino 114, *115*, *116*, 117
Monterey, USS, light carrier *91*
Montgomery, General Sir Bernard 56, 58, *58*, 62, 110, 111, 171, 177, 179, 180, 182, 188
Moscow 70, 74, *74*, 76, 77, 84
Mussolini, Benito, 22, 30, 82, 110, 111, *112*
Mutaguchi, General Renya 140, 143, 144

Nagasaki 136
Nagumo, Admiral Chuichi 95, 100, 123
Nevada, USS, battleship 100
New Guinea 95, 122, 127
New Zealand 15
  armed forces of 30, 114
Nimitz, Admiral Chester W *80*, 95, 122, 123, 130
Nishimura, Vice-Admiral Shoji 131
Norfolk, HMS, cruiser 38
Normandy, landings in 92, 170-1, *170-5*, 174, 176, 177, 179
North Africa 44-8, 54-9, 62-3, 83
  see also French North Africa
Norway 16, 17, *17*, 34
Nuremberg Rally, 1934 *13*

Ohio, US tanker 52, *52*
Okamura, General Yasuji 147
Okinawa 134, *135*

Oklahoma, USS 100
Operation Anvil 176
Operation Barbarossa 68, 70, 76, 77, 84
Operation Market Garden 180
Operation Overlord 170-4, 176
Operation Pedestal 52
Operation Sealion 26, 28
Operation Torch 60, *60-1*, 62
Orel 70
Ozawa, Vice-Admiral Jisaburo 128, 130-1

Pacific
  campaigns in 122-37
  prewar Japanese rivalry in 9
Paris, *1*, *23*, *81*, 177
Patch, Lieutenant General Alexander 176
Patton, General George S 110, 164, 176, 177, 182, 184
Paul, Prince, of Yugoslavia 29
Pearl Harbor 9, *78-9*, 84, 87, 89, *89*, 99-100, *99-100*, 103, 123
Pennsylvania, USS *100*
Percival, Lieutenant General A E 101
Perth, HMAS, cruiser 106
Pétain, Marshal Henri 22
Peter, King, of Yugoslavia 29
Philippine army 103
Philippine Islands 9, 89, 103-4, 127, 128, 130-2
Philippine Sea, Battle of 128
Pola, Italian cruiser 49
Poland 14-5, 80, 82, 160, 162
Polish Corridor 13, 80
Port Moresby 95, 122, 127, *127*
Pound, Admiral Sir Dudley 39
Pridham-Wippell, Vice-Admiral H D 49
Prince of Wales, HMS, battleship 38
Prinz Eugen, cruiser 38
propaganda 85, *85*

Quisling, Vidkun 16

Rabaul 122, 125
Ramsay, Admiral Sir Bertram 174
Rangoon 107, *138-9*, 140, 145
Reynaud, Paul 22
Rhine river 180, *181*, 182, 184, *184*, 186
Rhineland, 13, 80
Ribbentrop, Joachim von, 14
Rintelin, General von 110
Ritchie, General N M 54
Rodney, HMS, battleship 38
Rokossovsky, Marshal Konstantin 162
Rome *108-9*, 117, 119
Rommel, General Erwin 44, *44-5*, 46-7, 54, 56-7, 60, 62, 170, 174, 177
Roosevelt, President F D *80*, 176
Rostov 70
Royal Air Force 22, 26, 38, 49, 52, 101, 107, 168, 169
Royal Navy 16, 22, 26, 38, 49, 134
  Force H, 38, 49
  Mediterranean Fleet 49, *50-1*
Rumania 30
Rundstedt, Field Marshal Gerd von 21, 68, 170, 174, 177
Russo-Finnish War 66, 68, 72

Saipan 128
Salerno 111
Santa Cruz, Battle of 124
Saratoga, USS, carrier 99
Scandinavia 16
Scheer, pocket battleship 39
Schörner, Field Marshal Friedrich 160, 162, 164
Scoones, General G A P 143
Seeckt, General Hans von 12
Shaw, USS, destroyer *99*
Shima, Vice-Admiral K 131
Shoho, Japanese carrier 122
Shokaku, Japanese carrier 122, 128
Sicily 110, 111, 155

Singapore 101
Slim, General Sir William 107, 140, 143, 144, 145
Smolensk 70, 76, *77*, 156
Solomon Islands 95, 122, 124-5, *126*, 127
South Africa 30
Soviet air force 70, 154
Soviet army 66, *69*, 73, 76, *77*, *148-9*, *166-7*, 188, *188*
  in Finland, 66, *66*
  counter-offensive, winter 1941-42 76, 77, 84, 154
  at Stalingrad 150, 152-3
  Kursk battles 154-5
  advances in 1943 156
  relief of Leningrad 158
  Ukraine recovered 160
  1944 offensive 162
  liberation of Czechoslovakia 164
  advance to Berlin 188
  Second Baltic Front 158
  First Belorussian Front 162, 168
  Second Belorussian Front 162
  First Ukrainian Front 160, 162, *162*, 188
  Second Ukrainian Front 160
  Fourth Ukrainian Front *163*
  Kalanin Front 77
  Leningrad Front 158
  South-West Front 70, 77
  Steppe Front 155
  Trans-Caucasus Front 150
  Volkhov Front 158
  West Front 68, 77
  Fifth Army 70
  Sixth Army 154
  Seventh Army 66
  Thirteenth Army 66
  Twentieth Army 77
  Forty-seventh Army 162
  Sixty-second Army *151*
Soviet navy 77
Soviet Union 7, 77, 84, 85, 92, 179, 186
  and Finland 66
  and Poland 15
  non-aggression pact with Germany 14
  supplies to 39, 77, 154
Spencer, USS *34*
Stalin, Josef 14, 15, 68, 176
Stalingrad 84, 150, 152-3, *153*
Stilwell, General Joseph 107, 142, 145, 147
Stuka dive bomber 18, 82, *83*
Stumme, General G 58
submarine warfare 34-7, 39, 40-1, *83*, 92
Sudetenland 13
Suffolk, HMS, cruiser 38
Syfret, Vice-Admiral E N 52

Taiho, Japanese carrier 128
Takagi, Vice-Admiral 122
Taranto 49, 111
Tarawa 91, 133
Tennessee, USS, battleship 100
Tinian 128
Tirpitz, battleship 39
Tobruk 44, 46, 47, 48, *48*, 54, 58
Tojo, General Hideki 87
Tokyo 89, 133, *137*
Tripoli, Libya 62
Truscott, Major General Lucius 11 119
Tulagi, Solomon Islands 95, 122
Tunis, Tunisia 60, 62, 110
Turner, Rear Admiral R Kelly 124

U-boats *32-3*, 34-7, 39, 40-1, *41*, *83*
Ugaki, Vice-Admiral Matome 128
Ukraine 68, 70, 160, *161*
United States 41, 84, 85, 92
  and Battle of Atlantic 36-7
  and China 147
  and Vichy France 60
  Japanese rivalry with 7, 9, 87
  strategy in Pacific 91, 95
United States Army

in North Africa 60, *60*, 62
in Philippines 103, *105*
in Sicily/Italy 110-2, 114, 117, 119, *119*
in Far East, *145*, *146*
in North-West Europe 174, 176, 177, *178*, 179, 180, *181*, 182-4
troops of *37*, *108-9*, *145*, *146*
6 Army Group 176, 180
First Army 170, 174, 182, 184, 186
Third Army 164, 176, 177, 182, 184, 186
Fifth Army 111, 112, 117, 119
Sixth Army 130
Seventh Army 110, 176, 184
Ninth Army 180
Tenth Army 134
VI Corps 117
VIII Corps 182
XIV Corps 125
XV Corps 177
82nd Airborne Division 170, 180
101st Airborne Division 170, 180, 182, *183*
Merrill's Marauders *144*
United States Army Air Force 136, *168*
  Eighth Air Force 168, 169
  Twelfth Air Force *116*
  Fourteenth Air Force 147
United States Marines 91, 124-5, *125*, *126*, 133, *133*
  1st Marine Division 124
United States Navy *34*, 37, 91, 134
  Third Fleet 130
  Seventh Fleet 130, 131
  Pacific Fleet 87, 89, 99, 122, 123
  Task Force 38 130
  Task Force 58 128, *128*
Ushijima, General Mitsuru 134
Utah, USS, battleship 100

Versailles Treaty 12, 13, 80, *81*
Vesuvius, Mount *117*
Vietinghoff, General Heinrich von 112, 119
Vittorio Veneto, Italian battleship 49

Wainright, Lieutenant General Jonathan 103
Wake Island 99, 100
Warsaw 15, *15*, 162
Wavell, General Sir Archibald 30, 44, 106, 140, 142
Weichs, General M F von 150
West Virginia, USS, battleship 100
Weygand, General Maxime 22
Wingate, Brigadier General Orde 142, *142*

Yamamoto, Admiral Isoroku 123
Yamashita, Lieutenant General Tomoyuki 101, *101*, 131-2
Yamato, Japanese battleship *96-7*, 134, *135*
Yorktown, USS, carrier 122, 123
Yugoslavia 29, 30

Zara, Italian cruiser 49
Zhukov, Marshal Georgi 162, 188
Zuikaku, Japanese carrier 122, 131

Acknowledgements
The publishers would like to thank Adrian Hodgkins who designed this book and Ron Watson who compiled the index. The following agencies and individuals kindly supplied the photographs.
Bison Picture Library 2-3, 8, 9, 10-11, 17, 20-21, 23, 24 both, 40-41, 42-43, 47, 50-51, 64-65, 72-73, 73, 82, 83, 85 (all), 87, 101, 102, 106-107, 108-109, 112, 116 bottom, 137 right, 141, 153 top, 157, 149, 161, 181 top
Bison/IWM 48
Bundesarchiv 1, 13, 15, 25, 59, 61, 81, 178-179
Crown © 52, 138-139
Imperial War Museum 4-5, 6-7, 26, 28 both, 32-33, 44, 45, 55, 56-57, 57, 58-59, 60, 126 left, 134-135 bottom, 148-149, 155 top, 170-171, 172
Novosti Press Agency 66, 68, 74, 77, 151, 153 bottom, 155 bottom, 160, 162, 163, 165, 166-167, 188
Peter Newark's Historical Pictures 70-71
US Air Force 93, 95, 100 bottom, 115, 116 top, 118, 136, 142, 168, 186
US Army 53, 80, 89, 118, 119, 127, 130-131, 145, 146, 147, 178, 181 bottom, 183 both, 184 both
US Coast Guard 34-35, 132, 175-176, 176
US Marine Corps 125, 133
US National Archives 18, 30, 91, 100 top, 144
US Naval Historical Center 96-97
US Navy 36-37, 78-79, 99, 120-121, 124, 126 right, 128, 129, 134-135 top, 137 left, 173, 175
Dr Diosdado M Yap, Bataan Magazine 104-105, 105